MIME TIME

45
COMPLETE ROUTINES
FOR EVERYONE

by
Happy Jack
Feder

illustrated by
MARC
VARGAS

MERIWETHER PUBLISHING LTD.
Colorado Springs, Colorado

Meriwether Publishing Ltd., Publisher
Box 7710
Colorado Springs, CO 80933

Cover design: Tom Myers
Cover photography: Ted Zapel
Interior illustrations: Marc Vargas

© Copyright MCMXCII Meriwether Publishing Ltd.
Printed in the United States of America
Second Edition

Library of Congress Cataloging-in-Publication Data

Feder, Happy Jack.
    Mime time / Happy Jack Feder : illustrated by Marc Vargas. -- 2nd ed.
      p.   cm.
    ISBN 0-916260-73-9 : $10.95
    1. Pantomimes. I. Title.
PN6120.P3F37 1992
792.3--dc20   92-25611
                                                CIP

For Mike,
occasional, unwitting partner in adventure,
and constant friend

Table of Contents

minded worker. What's a widget and why is it doing all those terrible things to me? Funny or valiant? One or two mimes.

EXTRA!! EXTRA!! READ ALL ABOUT IT!!

You're now the lucky owner of *Mime Time!* It's filled with forty-five fully detailed mime routines that can quickly be put to use by you and all other would-be and professional mimes. That's right! Whether you're a seasoned pro, an ambitious beginner, a theater student, an occasional dabbler in the performing arts, or just an unlucky club member who has been assigned to do a mime routine at the upcoming talent show, *Mime Time* is a handy, useful book. Read on and see why you won't be wrapping fish in it!

Sound Advice for the Soundless Performer

The first section (Technique—and Then Some) offers tips and ideas to help the beginner get off the ground and onto the stage: how to use the book, apply makeup, practice, make props, etc. This valuable information will help all lost beginners find the door to the theater.

Routines for the Single Performer

There are dozens of routines in this section that can be performed by the lone mime! Each one has been tried and tested on stage, and each one is a winner. Just follow the instructions and you'll have your audience laughing, weeping, or pondering the meaning of life. Your choice.

Routines for Two or More Performers

Since many mimes work in groups, you'll need routines specifically written to be performed by two or more people. You've come to the right place to find them. And if you should ever happen to get tired of working with a partner, why, lucky you!

You'll be able to adapt many of the routines in this section for use by one performer.

Note: Naturally, you can perform any routine whether you're a boy, man, girl, or woman—regardless of the sex of the character(s)!

TECHNIQUE —
AND THEN SOME

IT'S A COVER UP!

Before you walk out on stage, you're going to want to look like a mime. Follow these instructions and, if you don't pass for the real thing, you'll at least squeak by as a distant relative.

Nothing to it, right? Right. Once you go through the procedure a few more times, there'll be less than nothing to it! Remember, this is a fairly traditional mime face that is presented. Many of the more modern mimes would even consider it a bit old-fashioned. Feel free to experiment with more or less makeup, searching for a face that fits your fancy. There's no law that says this is THE FACE, and that, without it, you aren't A REAL MIME.

Brenda Bounce, Juggling Mime of Montana, sports a clean face. Washed with soap or wiped with a damp rag, a clean face makes for easier makeup application. And, if you're like Brenda Bounce and can't quite scrub off those freckles, well, read on!

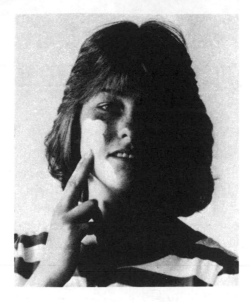

Brenda Bounce dips her *fingertips* into a cannister or tube of whiteface (available in magic stores or theatrical supply houses) and rubs it on her face. Small circular motions seem to do the best job.

All done! Nary a freckle to be seen! Notice how she put the whiteface over her eyebrows. Down at the other end, she stopped at the jawline. And although it's not necessary, she gives her face a light dusting of powder. This helps soften some lines, reduce glare, and solidify the sometimes greasy, runny (especially when under bright, hot lights!) whiteface.

With a heavy, black eyeliner pencil, Brenda Bounce draws a line around her entire face. This serves to separate the face from the rest of the body, allowing her expressions to be more distinct and focused.

A little more liner around the mouth makes it seem bigger and provides high contrast with the surrounding sea of whiteface.

The final touch, the eyes! Brenda Bounce goes for the simple touch here. Some mimes are more elaborate, adding
heavy eyebrows, little tears, wider eyes, stars, even freckles!
(But having just covered her freckles, Brenda Bounce finds
such additional touches to be redundant.) When she's finished her show, Brenda Bounce will clean off with a cold
cream and soap and water.

TECHNICAL EDUCATION OF A MIME

While this book provides you with enough successful material to perform several shows, thereby solving the biggest part of your problems, you still may be worried about the smaller part of the problem: How do I learn the technical skills of performing mime? As long as you are sincere in your determination to learn, the task is a simple and enjoyable one.

The ideal way to learn technical skills is to enroll in a mime class. These are offered as several day seminars, university classes, or adult/alternative education classes. The big advantage in taking a class is that you get to work with other people. You learn not only by watching and criticizing others, but by having more people watch and criticize you!

If there are no classes available to you, don't despair. You can always teach yourself! Remember, mime is nothing more than the telling of stories without sound and without props. All actions and gestures are no different from those you would perform during a normal day.

The only difference is that as a mime, you want to make the actions and gestures _clearly defined_. You can do this by exaggerating an action, executing it more slowly than in real life, and focusing all your attention on the one action and not allowing others to compete with it.

How do you know if you're doing it right? Simple. Perform in front of an audience! Even a few friends or relatives will be able to give you a pretty good critique. If they like what they see, you're ready for the big time.

Remember, all the practice and education in the world is nothing compared to the value of a single public performance. Experience is your best teacher. Each show you give will add to your abilities to get a little bit bigger laugh, draw a longer sigh, and squeeze a few more tears from the people in the audience.

How to Use Props

Ah, props! The average mime starts out thinking how wonderful it is to tell a story without sound or props, just the action of his or her body. Before long, though, the mime's thinking how nice it would be to use a widget here, a gizmo there, and a whatchamacallit in the background. He or she has turned a simple thing into a full-fledged theater production!

There's no right or wrong when it comes to using props in mime. It's a matter of personal choice. Most mimes do use at least a few simple props, however. A table and a chair are popular props (it's tough to fake sitting down!).

If you decide to use additional props, make sure they are simple and nondescript. All you want in a good prop is the *form* of the object. For instance, a straight, black stick makes a much better cane than one with a curved handle of carved ivory. A good prop is an *aid* to the mime, not a distraction.

Staging

There are more *things* to consider than the stage props you'll be using. There are the elements which surround your show: lighting, music, special effects, and title cards.

Only the title cards should be considered a necessity, with the others being optional.

A title card is usually a large sheet of cardboard (18" x 26") with the title of the skit written on it. Before the skit begins, either you or an assistant displays the title card to the audience. When they see "THE ICE CREAM CON," they'll know the skit is about ice cream and trickery. This is helpful in getting the audience on the right track so they won't spend the first few moments trying to figure out what the skit is all about. Displaying the title card is also a nice way of putting borders on your skits. It gives you and the audience a chance to breathe and prepare for the next skit.

Lights? Worry about them only if you're on a professional stage that is already equipped with lights. The most common problem in lighting a stage for mime is that the whiteface makeup tends to produce very harsh shadows directly beneath the eyes and nose. Aim your lights from the sides and the very front as much as possible to avoid this problem.

The addition of music to your show can produce some wonderful moments. Most importantly, it helps break the continuous pressure of silence. Audiences appreciate a little variety. Be careful to use the music sparingly, however. You don't want to perform an entire skit to a piece of music (except under very special circumstances). Another thing to consider is the added mechanical complication of using music. Do you want to carry a sound system, as well as an assistant, to every performance?

Special effects (flashing lights, special noises, custom-built sets) are of concern only to the more experienced mimes who have a strong interest in professional theater. For the average mime, most special effects are more trouble and money than they are worth.

Lighting, title cards, music, and special effects are all basically optional considerations (with title cards being strongly urged). If you're a beginner, don't worry about these extras until you've gained some experience in basic mime.

Each skit in this book has instructions, when called for, on special lighting, music, and effects. These instructions can for the most part be considered optional.

Where and When? Here and Now!

How to perform a mime routine is a question easily answered: Use this book for performance material and combine with your own practice and enthusiasm. *Who* is to perform is also a simple question: YOU! You're the one reading this book and investigating the possibility of performing because you want to be involved in theater, you want to create, you want to earn your own self-satisfaction—and you'd like others to applaud you in the process. But *where* and *when* to actually climb on a stage is often a more difficult matter with which to come to grips.

The beginner thinks that the premier performance is when one lays it all on the line, that it's a make-or-break, do-or-die experience. Sigh . . . Such is not the case. *Every* performance, especially the first ones of beginning mimes who are still struggling with their technical skills, should be considered a learning, growing experience. Armed with such knowledge, the matter of where and when to perform is a snap to figure. *Here* and *now*! After all, why should you wait to learn? To increase your skills, stage savvy, sense of confidence, personal rewards? Quit standing around.

Take your skills and find a stage. If your skills be meager, start with humble surroundings: family get-togethers, parks, pizza and ice cream parlors, birthday and office parties. There's little pressure in these situations to WOW the audience. People don't expect to see the world's greatest mime while munching pizza and quaffing beer. Performing on a real stage in front of a seated audience that expects a Good Show in return for Good Money can be tough for a beginner's psyche.

As time goes by, you'll learn at which types of places you like to perform, and how frequently you like to perform. But that's later. Right now, hurry and start performing!

From Humble Hunkerings . . .

A final, emphatic reminder for the budding/would-be professional mime: Start out small! Keep your ambition in check, strive for attainable goals, and take one step at a time. All too often, beginners (especially in the entertainment biz) get starry-eyed dreaming about eventual fame and success. This results in either nothing being accomplished (too busy dreaming, wishing) or in the accomplishment of a big flop (the biting off of more than one can chew). Both result in another mime who gets soured on the profession and quits. (Pass the hankie! This is too much to bear!)

Progress carefully in developing all aspects of mime (props, places to perform, material to practice, etc.) This isn't to say you shouldn't challenge yourself; it *is* to say: Don't knock yourself out! You'll amaze yourself with the results of continual, steadfast labors.

Each Mime to His or Her Own

Have you ever read a book or short story, get to the end of it and say to yourself, "*If I had written it, I would have done it differently. . . .*"? Of course you have.

Now's your chance to tailor a story to suit yourself. The mime stories presented in this book are by no means cast in iron or etched in stone. If you don't like a particular something, *change it!* Want to change a suggested melancholy mood to a silly, happy one? Consider it done. Want to see the kid in "THE ICE CREAM

CON" get his just desserts? Then don't let him get a second cone.

While these stories are complete, fully detailed, and entirely entertainable to audiences, they are also malleable frameworks waiting for a unique individual (like yourself) to put his or her own stamp to them.

Get to it.

Teamwork

Being alone isn't always fun. More often, it's better to share experiences with others. When it comes to painting your face and wiggling your body in front of a bunch of strangers, in hopes of entertaining them, it's definitely comforting to have the shoulders of a partner or two to lean on.

Before committing yourself to a team effort, here are a few questions you and your compatriots should answer, lest your friendships quickly and irreversibly sour. Can everyone practice together at the same time (and is it necessary)? Who's in charge when big decisionmaking is at hand? For instance, what if one wants uniform uniforms and others want variety, or one wants the group to drive 300 miles for a show and the others want to watch tv? How often will the group perform? Can individuals perform as such outside the group? Who decides which material will be performed? Who decides *how* it will be performed? If the group splits (as ninety-nine percent of such groups always do), who owns the name of the group? Does everyone have the same short- and long-term goals: to make money, to make art, to travel the world, to do local birthday parties, to do tv specials, or to cut LP mime albums?

The most important question to be answered is: Can an otherwise solid friendship stay outside of and survive a disastrous professional relationship?

Remember: Mime should be fun for both the audience and the performers. Don't subjugate the fun to the often strenuous demands of teamwork.

YOUR HOSTS

After discussing what to watch out for in teamwork, let's meet the team to watch *for*: The Smiling Leper Players! They'll be your hosts from here on, leading you through one routine after another. Their diversity and talent shows up first in the name they chose for themselves. "Smiling" is for the happy side of life they show, "Leper" for the tragic. Together, these words create a perplexing irony that the players try to present and untangle for the viewer.

GOING SOLO
(FOR A VERY,
VERY HIGH)

Wally Says:

A fun routine (especially to practice!). It's your option when it comes to switching characters. Personally, I think it works better when you *do* switch.

The Ice Cream Con

Unanswered Questions?

Little Boy Wally is walking along the street when he comes across an ice cream store. Mmmm! He rubs his tummy and licks his lips. Although he can barely reach the doorknob, he manages to turn it. The door, pushed by Wally's leaning weight, flies open, spilling him on the floor. Embarrassed, he quickly gets up and brushes himself clean.

Wally goes to the ice cream counter, where he has to stand on his toes to see the many different flavors. When he puts his hands on the glass divider, the man behind the counter yells at him. Wally quickly removes his hands and sheepishly wipes the glass clean with his sleeve. After watching the man turn away, he checks to see that no one else is watching him. All clear! He quickly and deliberately smears his hands across the glass. When the man suddenly turns around, Wally snaps his hands away and pretends to be casually scratching his ear. *Who, me? No, I wasn't touching the glass. Gimme a break, huh?*

Favored Flavors

The man turns away again, and Wally sticks his tongue out at him before getting down to the serious business of choosing a flavor. And just look at all those flavors! One makes Wally's eyes glow and his mouth water (he wipes it clean, though), and another almost makes him puke! Who creates these weird flavors, anyway?

A decision is finally reached. The man is called back. *This one!* The man grabs a scoop and a cone, reaches down and carves out a ball of ice cream. *Not one scoop, mister, two!* What!? The man is scooping the wrong flavor!

Wally pounds the glass and stomps his feet and . . . oops. He slowly pulls his hands away from the glass divider, looking apologetically at the man.

Wally points to a different flavor, the man starts to scoop—*no, wait, this one! No, I mean that one! Er, maybe that one on the end. I changed my mind, I want the one on the other end . . .*

Wally jumps and shudders as the man yells for him to make up his mind. He shuts his eyes, spins, and blindly points at a flavor. YICK! Wally starts to change his mind again, but figures he's better off if he remains silent.

Coins for Cones

Wally reaches for the ice cream cone, grinning from ear to ear. He lunges for it—but his fingers grasp thin air as the man pulls it away from Wally's hand. *What the . . . ?* Ah, money first.

Wally digs deep into his pocket, pulls out a coin and puts it on the counter. *Not enough?* He pulls out another coin.

Wally digs deep into his pocket, pulls out a coin, and puts it on the counter. *Not enough?* He pulls out a coin from the other pocket. *Still not enough?* Another coin from another pocket and WHAT!? More?

Wally steps back and suspiciously eyes the man. *What's the ice cream made from, anyway? Chicken milk?* Reluctantly, he pulls out a checkbook and writes a check. *Take all my money, you ice cream robber baron!* Wally exchanges the check for the cone and turns around a happier human.

Three-Scream Warranty Offered

Wally stares rapturously at the beeeautiful cone. He reaches out to lick it, but thinks of something and stops. *Is anyone looking?* No. Wally deliberately dumps the two scoops on the floor,

smiles, takes a deep breath and starts to cry, louder and louder with each wail!

The man finally notices Wally and calls him over to the counter, where he presents him with a new ice cream cone. The tears vanish. Wally reaches for the cone, hesitates, and decides to push his luck. *One more scoop, please?* It's a close call, but the man gives it to him. Wally takes the cone, thanks the man, turns around and . . . picks up the two scoops from the floor and stacks them on his new cone!

He snickers with delight, takes a quick lick, sees that the man is getting angry, and hightails it away!

The Cowpoke

Saddle Up!

Cowpoke Larry walks up to his horse with his hands on his gunbelt and legs bowed from years of shining the saddle. He stops and pats ol' Ricochet on the forehead, then readjusts his ten-gallon Stetson. He picks up a saddle, flings it over the top of Ricochet, and quickly secures it.

Ol' Larry spits out a wad he's been chawin' on for the last week or so. It kinda drizzles down his chin and he has to wipe it clean with his sleeve.

He pulls out a bag of 'baccy and deftly rolls a slim one. He strikes a match off his rough whiskers, lights up, takes a big puff and—coughs! *Waugh! I didn't have problems smoking when I was five years old. Why now?* He recovers and sticks the cigarette in the very corner of his lips.

Mount Up, Swallow Down

Larry quits pokin' around and tries to mount ol' Ricochet. He grabs the horn of the saddle and lifts his boot to the stirrup. Almost, that is. His legs aren't as limber as they once were. He's forced to lift his foot with his hands (after checking to see that no one is watching). *Darn horses are taller than I remember them being.*

After a few tries, he swings his other leg over the top. There! Back on the saddle again!

Cowpoke Larry readjusts his cigarette and lightly slaps the reigns. Ricochet gets spooked and rears up, giving Larry quite a fright. He eventually calms the horse and reaches for his cigarette. Oops. It's not in his lips. His hand follows a line down his throat to his stomach. He gulps and makes a face.

Out on the Range

Larry's too busy a cowpoke to spend any more time worrying about a little ol' cigarette, of all things! The sun's almost up and there's work to do! He gives Ricochet a slap and takes off down the trail. Larry bounces roughly on the saddle, much to his discomfort. Why, the ride is so bumpy he has to push his hat down to prevent it from falling off!

Larry eventually settles down to a smoother pace. He stops, perches high on the saddle, and surveys the lay of the land. He's looking closely for stray cows. All he sees is prairie and sagebrush. Might not be a hard day after—*Hold yer horses! Gol' darn if there ain't a stray out there after all!*

He pulls his lariat off the saddle and twirls a big loop. *C'mon Ricochet! Git a move on!*

Round Up Mix Ups

Cowpoke Larry's equestrian skills have seen better days. Ricochet bounces him a few feet in the air with each gallop. Larry's head is jiggling faster than a working woodpecker's! As they approach the stray cow, Larry starts to slide off the saddle, despite his best efforts. Realizing what's going to happen, he decides to better his chances by jumping off and tumbling to the ground in a cloud of dust.

OOF! They sure don't make the ground as soft as they use ta!

It's a long moment before Larry gets the strength to pick himself up, and when he does, he moves stiffly, painfully. He spits the dust out of his mouth, brushes his clothes clean, and pulls a few thistles out of his rear end. He picks up the lariat and looks for Ricochet. She's off and running. Larry dismisses her with a wave of his hand: *Go on and git, then, you ol' pack o' bones!*

All Tied Up (and Down)

Larry spots the cow and readies the lariat. He steals up on it and throws the twirling lariat with all his might.

Some days it's better not to wake up.

Larry has succeeded in capturing himself in the lariat. He can scarcely move. Frustrated as all git out, he reels off a string of cuss words. Glancing over his shoulder to make sure none of his cowboy compatriots are about (they'd never let him live this down), he falls to the ground and twists and squirms like a snake. Humiliating, but a cowpoke does what a cowpoke's gotta.

As if to make up for lost time, he jumps to his feet and starts madly swinging the lariat. But what do you know! The cow walks right up to Larry and starts licking him. *Aw, shucks!* Larry rolls his eyes and tenderly slips the loop over the cow's head. *C'mon, foller me.*

A Fireside Discussion

Some time later they reach their destination. Larry ties the cow to a post and makes a (little) fire. He gathers the wood, strikes a match, and fans the fire into huge flames. It's so hot he has to step back to wipe his brow. He turns to the cow and beckons with his finger.

Come on over here, Bessie, I ain't a gonna hurt you.

Bessie knows better. Irritated, Larry puts his hands on his hips and struts over to her. He points to the fire, but she doesn't budge. *Why do I always get stuck doing things the hard way?*

He bends over and, with all the strength he can muster, lifts her up. He staggers about with the enormous load and (miraculously not falling over) makes his way to the fire where he plops her down—and plops his tired self on top of her.

Phew! They sure don't make cows as light as they used to!

The Brand of Success

After Larry catches his breath, he quietly and secretly grabs the branding iron. He sticks it in the coals and gives it a few twirls. Lifting it out, he touches his finger to the end. *YEEOWW! Just right.*

He turns, stealthily, and finds a spot on Bessie to mark the brand. She catches on and puts up a hellacious fight. It's rough-

and-tumble for a while, and Larry can't tell up from down. The fight ends up in a stalemated knot of man and cow—which Larry thinks is to his advantage. He grabs the branding iron, aims, and shoves down hard with all his strength (what's left of it).

His mouth falls open and his body freezes, motionless. Shocked with his success? No. He turns and looks at his own hind end and sees a smoldering brand mark. After this sinks into his weatherworn, leathered brain, he shouts and grabs his posterior.

Last anyone heard of Cowpoke Larry, he was highstepping for the nearest waterhole.

Molly Says:

I've been practicing this one for years and still can't get that ball to do what I want! Hope you have better luck.

The Magic Ball

Losers Winners, Finders Weepers

Molly happily trots out to center stage, smiles, and takes a deep, joyful breath. *What a wonderful day to be alive and have some fun! What a fantabulous . . . say . . . ?*

Molly's attention is grabbed by a ball bouncing across the stage. She adroitly grabs it before it passes her. Holding it up for examination, she sees it is an average ball, a few inches in diameter. She looks back to where it came. *No one there seems to have lost it. Might as well keep it and have some fun!*

She starts out with the simple stuff and bounces it back and forth from hand to hand, laughing and having a grand old time. Giving the ball a definite backspin, she flicks it forward and catches it. Now she bounces it on one knee, then the other, then back and forth. Giving the ball one last bounce, she sends it over her shoulder and behind her back. In the nick of time she ever so casually kicks it back to her hands with the bottom of her foot.

Ball of a Different Bounce

She bounces it again—only this time the ball doesn't bounce. *What's going on?* The ball remains motionless on the ground. She scratches her head, picks it up, tries again to bounce it—and again it falls flat, splat, smack motionless. *Hmm.*

She tries again, giving the ball a good, swift throw. *OUCH!* It bounces back and hits her in the forehead! How do you like that? She's stunned for a moment but soon recovers and finds the ball still bouncing in front of her. She reaches for it and it bounces to the left, out of her grasp. She reaches again and it bounces, forward. She's now chasing the ball all over the place, always one bounce behind the darn thing. Quite fed up and frustrated, she abandons the chase and sets her hands on her hips. She raises a hand of warning when lo and behold! The ball bounces politely into her hands. *I'm not going crazy. I'm not going crazy. I am NOT going crazy!*

More of the Same, with Variations

She almost starts bouncing the ball again when she thinks better of it and hesitates. This time she'll throw the ball through the air! She executes several fancy throws, never letting the ball bounce, and never letting it get too far away from her. Just for the heck of it, she throws the ball straight up in the air—pretty high!

Then she throws it even higher! One more time, HIGHER! She holds her hands out to catch it.

Now what?

The ball doesn't return. It's sort of stuck up there.

She tightens her lips and patiently (or is it impatiently?) taps her foot. Impatience defeats patience, and she tries to jump up and grab the ball! No luck. A few more tries and she realizes she's licked. She gives up and starts to leave.

Klunk, klunk, klunk. . . .

She stops, turns around, and sees the ball bouncing. She quickly lunges for it, only to see it move horizontally! The ball floats (flies?) a few feet above the ground, shooting back and forth, causing Molly to dodge it a few times.

Sheesh! What did I ever do to deserve this?

The ball finally flies out of sight. Molly breathes a sigh of relief and wipes her hands clean of the entire affair. Off to a new adventure!

Back for More

SMACK! The ball returns, slamming into the side of her head. *Enough is ENOUGH!*

Molly glares angrily at the ball, now bouncing innocently enough in front of her. She lunges for it, misses, and falls to the ground—where her hand lands on a stick.

A stick . . . Hmm. Worth a try.

She picks the stick up and holds it like a bat, locates the bouncing ball, and swings with an intensity that would have put Babe Ruth to shame. That ball is gone! Molly even pulls out a pair of binoculars to watch its flight.

She turns to walk away and finds the ball bouncing in front of her. *AARGH!*

She leaps for it, wrestles it to the ground, and lets her frustration and anger get the better of her. She bites into it! *Chomp, chomp chomp! That settles that!*

She gets up, smiles, burps, and walks away . . . with a most distinctive little *bounce*.

Wally Says:

Find yourself a drum and teach your partner to play a simple, sad, lonely military beat, preferably while hidden behind a curtain. If you're without a partner, make a tape recording you can use. The drums aren't necessary, but they're sure a nice touch.

A Soldier's Story

Hanging Out

(The drum sounds, the stage is empty. Wally walks out and the drum fades away.)

Wally Boy the teenager is trucking down the avenue, slouched over, chewing gum, and pushing his long hair out of his face. He's bored. *This is a drag. Too much hang time.*

His study of discontentment is disturbed when someone calls to him. *Who, me?* Bewildered, he nonchalantly walks over to the man who called to him. The man is seated behind a table that Wally leans against. Wally looks things over, listens, nods his head. He can't help grin and raise his hand in a sloppy mock salute: *Go on, you don't want me!?*

The man at the table, an army recruiter, does indeed want Wally. Wally starts to walk away, but the man calls him back. He says something that makes Wally think more carefully. Wally incredulously rubs his forefinger and thumb together. *Money? You'll shell out bucks for me to play soldier boy?*

He checks his pockets and verifies what he already knows. Empty. He shrugs his shoulders: *Why not?* He bends down to the table and signs the forms. Putting the pen down, he stands in a moment of silent, private thought and once again brushes his long hair out of his face.

You're in the Army Now

(The drum sounds and time passes.)

Wally is now in basic training camp going through a rigorous exercise. He's pooped! Can't even keep his tongue in his mouth! He somehow manages to continue doing pushups, situps, running in place, and crawling under wires and over fences.

When he finishes, he barely has the strength to salute his sergeant. The sergeant yells at him and he squints. Somehow, he finds the strength to do it right.

Getting Down to Business

(Time passes and the drum sounds.)

Wally is learning to use a rifle. He lifts it to his shoulder and takes aim. The tension builds as his finger quivers on the trigger. BANG! The recoil knocks him to the ground. Undaunted, he picks up the rifle and tries again, wincing at the commands of his supervisor.

The next stage of his training is to fix a bayonet to the end of his gun and use it in simulated combat. Wally tests the sharpness of the tip of the blade.

Ouch! No one said anything about pain!

He readies himself and charges forward, thrusting out the bayonet. Plop! He trips and falls on his nose. He gets up slowly and walks away, rubbing his nose. His body is stiff and tired and his pricked finger hurts.

Lotta fun this is!

The New Will

(Time passes and the drum sounds.)

Wally goes through his exercises again. The little teenager has been replaced by a tough, steel-edged man. There's a sparkle in his eyes and a proud sense of accomplishment in the way he stands.

Rifle practice is perfect. Sharp, even, with only the slightest indication of recoil.

The bayonet charges forward like a rocket, slash, slash, stab!

Wally jumps to attention, twirls his rifle in a deft series of moves, and assumes an "at ease" stance. He stares straight ahead, unafraid, not the least bit tired. His jaw is like iron—but

he permits himself a very small, almost indiscernible smile to cross his face.

He salutes and turns.

Read All About It

(Time passes and the drum sounds.)

Wally is walking along a city street in full uniform, tall and proud. He waves to a few people. A man stops him to shake his hand. Wally reaches up to wipe the long hair out of his face, only to find a short stubble. He chuckles until something catches his eye.

He hurries to a newspaper stand, puts a coin in the slot, and reads the front page. WAR!

Wally turns and looks angrily to the east. He grimaces, grits his teeth, and shakes his fist at his new enemy. He rolls the paper into a ball, throws it to the ground, and puts his hands on his hips. He's ready!

Laughs and Whatnot

(Time passes and the drum sounds.)

Wally and his buddies are in action now, walking down a road with their rifles, nervous and tense. Wally thinks he sees something and he jumps. *Ha! Just a bird! How about that, guys? Tweet, tweet, fly away, fly away!*

They laugh. Wally lights a cigarette, passes it to a friend, lights another for himself, and lets it hang from the corner of his mouth. Wally gets an idea and smiles. He pretends to shoot his gun at an imaginary enemy and urges his friends to join in. They finish and the laughter subsides. He swallows and nervously bites his lip. *What the hell am I doing here, anyway?*

A sudden explosion sends him tumbling. He jumps up and BOOM! another explosion. He falls flat and waits for the air to settle. After a moment he slowly gets to his knees and wipes his brow. He starts to chuckle and say something to his buddies. Then he realizes that they are dead. He tries to shake life back into one but gets no response. He lets the body drop and sees that his own hands are covered with their blood. Embarrassed, he wipes them on his pants. When he starts to wipe at a tear in his eye, another explosion sends him tumbling. He grabs his gun and shoots wildly for a brief moment. He can't see the enemy.

One last glance at his dead buddies. *Sorry, guys, gotta run.*

Tit for Tat

(Time passes and the drum sounds.)

Wally is exhausted. He's had little or no rest these last few days, and it shows. He stumbles along, dazed and disoriented. He lifts his canteen, unscrews the cap, and takes a sip—but there's no water. He snarls and tosses it aside.

A noise!

Where?

Over there, again!

He crouches down and readies his rifle, slipping the bayonet on the end. He stalks forward, cautious. He turns. *THE ENEMY!* Wally charges with his bayonet, but the enemy dodges. They jump back and forth, slashing, evading. Wally seems to gain the advantage and steadily forces the enemy offstage. Wally follows, and for a moment, the stage is empty. Wally returns, walking slowly and his head hanging low. Concentrating on what he has just done, he absently cleans the bayonet with his shirtsleeve.

The Final Peace

Wally lights a cigarette and puts it between his lips. He's so tired. He'd like to take a nap. *For about a thousand years.*

He hears another noise but doesn't react with his previous alacrity. He's too weary to move fast. When he sees the cause of the noise, he drops his rifle. It's the enemy. A lot of them. He turns to run but finds he's surrounded. He falls to his knees, a broken man, begging for mercy.

An enemy soldier walks forward and stands directly over Wally, who now bites the back of his hand, shaking. Wally's eyes widen. Something is happening. Wally doesn't want to watch.

He covers his face.

(Lights abruptly go black and the drum sounds.)

Surf's Up

Hot Feet

Carla the Beach Bum scoots her little car into a tight (tight as in "close your eyes to make it fit") parking space and slams into the brake pedal. *Like Radical, totally out.*

She hops out, kicks the door shut, and unstraps a long, heavy surfboard from the roof rack. Tucking it under her arm, she blocks the sun from her eyes and checks out the wave action. *Lookin' good, lookin' good.*

She darts out across the sandy beach. Her feet sink into the fine sand and slow her progress . . . which wouldn't be so bad if the sand weren't so *hot!* Carla lifts one foot to brush away the brimstone and blow it with some cool air. She then does the

same to the other foot. Back and forth she goes, never quite fast enough. Knowing when to cut her losses, she grits her teeth and sprints for the water. *Ahhhhhh!*

A Slick Proposition

After reaching the water, Carla plants her board into the soft ground, nose down. *Yep! Waves are good, getting better.*

She takes a bar of wax from her pocket, sets the board flat, and begins her work. With long, sweeping motions she rubs the wax onto the board. It's hard work, especially for a surfer. *Whew!* She stops to catch her breath and wipe the sweat from her brow. She looks at her hands. YIKES! The ends of her fingers are missing! Has she rubbed them off?

A more careful inspection reveals that they are merely cramped inward. She painfully curls her fingers back to their original condition.

The waves beckon. *The heck with this wax action, I'm going surfing!* The remaining sliver of wax is tossed aside as Carla charges ever onward.

Chilling Prospects

Not *too* far into the water, however. She stops motionless in a few inches of the wet stuff, teeth gritted, body tight. *Cold city!* Shaking with spasms of shivers, Carla employs the slow and gradual method of temperature adjustment. She splashes small handfuls of water to small portions of the body.

Oh, the heck with this business, too!

Nose pinched, she dives in and submerges her entire body. She jumps up, shakes her head briskly, and catches her breath, then smiles. *All done!*

In Search of the Perfect Wave

Carla moves into deeper water, now standing on her toes. She climbs atop her board and assumes a kneeling position. When she paddles, her board has a tendency to veer to the right. She corrects this by occasionally doubling up on the right-hand paddles. Now out in the ocean proper, gentle undulating waves keep her in a constant rocking motion.

She pokes her head up as high as possible to scout the horizon. *Here comes a wave . . . a big wave . . . a real . . . big . . .* Dazzled by its size, she waits too long to get out of its way. SMASH! BASH! And CRASH! The wave sends poor pretty Carla tumbling, spinning, flopping, and flipping, barely able to hold onto her board or her breath. When the wave finally passes her by, she climbs on her board and breathes a sincere sigh of relief.

Time for her to do it to it! Carla sits on the board and turns it so she'll be ready for a ride. Here comes another wave! She begins paddling to gain speed. Faster, faster! The swelling water approaches! Faster! Here's the wave! Up she goes! Up, up! And then down, down. *Bummer! I missed a ride on a perfectly tailored wave!* She watches the wave break past her with more than a slight trace of frustration.

Surf's Way Up!

Waiting for the next (next? FIRST!) ride seems to take a terribly long time. What with the sun's rays beating down on her back, the sound of distant breakers, and the gentle, peaceful rocking of the water, Carla gets a little drowsy-eyed. She yawns, stretches back on the board, and—*TIDAL WAVE!*

It's a monster wave! A huge wave! A coming-her-way wave! She spins around and paddles for her life. She's a hummingbird on water. One quick glance behind, and up . . . and up . . . the wave is here! She's caught a ride!

Carla quits paddling and rises on one foot, struggling to maintain a delicate balance. Miraculously, she stands on two feet. Time for an ear-to-ear grin. *Hey, this is some kinda fun!*

Carla works the wiggles and wobbles out of the board and brings it under a smooth form of control. She's having a ball. *Dip to the left, dip to the right, hang ten, slide in and out of the curl, shoot through the tube, climb high and drop down for a rush of speed! Get Radical!*

Clowning around, she does a somersault and almost rolls off the end. *What fun. Now for a handstand . . .*

Carla looks between her legs at the wave, almost as if for the first time. She stands and turns around. It is a big wave. *I've been riding that?*

In an instant she loses control and falls off the board. She's once again tossed and churned, bounced and turned. BOING! The wave spits her out into the air. She looks down and gasps. She covers her eyes and gasps. CRUNCH! She lands on the ground.

Surf's Out

Time passes.

Carla finally manages to sit up, slightly dazed, and spit some water out of her mouth. She absently starts paddling again, only to discover she's on good old terra firma. Suddenly, she jumps up! *What was that?* She turns around to find that her surfboard has landed beside her, nose in the ground. She picks it up, turns again . . . ! She claps her hand to her forehead in surprise. Her car! She straps the board to the roof rack, climbs inside, and casts a last glance at the ocean waves before driving away.

Playtime!

Starting Up, Starting Right

Little Molly wakes up early in the morning, peels off the bed covers, and jumps into high gear. She's a little too old to be called a toddler, too young for school. One way or the other, she doesn't care. She quickly dresses, but gets stuck with the shoe dilemma. *Left or right? And how do you tie these laces? This is stupider than having to go to bed at night!*

She throws the shoes and laces into a corner and stomps out to the kitchen. *Breakfast!* Being the short little gal that she is, she has to reach high for everything. Eventually, the bowl, spoon, cereal box, and milk carton end up on the table. She pours more milk and cereal into the bowl than it can hold. Molly's not bothered. Her idea of cleaning up is to smear the mess around with her hands. The cereal in the bowl is quickly gobbled and the milk slurped. After wiping her mouth clean and burping, she steps outside into the bright sunlight, squinting.

Speed Demon

Outside! Playtime! Molly runs to her tricycle and peddles away. What fun! She zigzags down the sidewalk and pretends to be a race driver. *Zoom! Zoom! Zoom! Full speed away, torpedoes ahead! Zoom! . . . Whoaaa!*

She tips over and falls to the grass. She's in shock, trying to figure out what happened. Then, with a deep breath, she begins to wail at full volume, continuing only until she realizes no one is watching. She turns off the tears just as abruptly as they started.

Nature in Action

She starts to get back on the tricycle when something on the ground catches her attention. She peers down for a closer investigation. It's a bug. Following it along at its slow but steady pace, Molly pokes it with her little finger. *Ook!* She shivers, makes a face, and giggles.

Carefully, she picks the bug up and changes its direction of travel. *This is fun!* Molly puts it in the palm of her hand and lets it crawl up her arm. As the bug nears her shoulder, she flicks it off with a snap of a finger. She walks over to where it landed and . . . stomps it flat. *Ook!*

Where She Stops, Nobody Knows

Molly joins some friends and shares an exciting idea: *Let's spin!* Without hesitation they begin spinning in circles. Molly's arms are stretched out and she occasionally caroms off a friend. It doesn't take long for the desired effect to be achieved. She stops and tries to stand perfectly still, but, dizzied, falls to her knees laughing.

All of a sudden, Molly doesn't feel so good. She crawls over to her tricycle and slowly peddles away, absently waving good-by to her friends.

What's All the Fuss?

A little bit of peddling works wonders for Molly. Once again she's grinning and zipping about with zest. Up ahead, she sees

another friend. She stops and talks with the friend. *What? Huh-uh! Yes! No. I don't know. Do what? My pants? Okay, I guess. I mean, I don't know. You first.*

In turn, Molly pulls her pants open. She looks at her friend, then at herself.

Big deal. See ya later.

The Nipping of a Budding Baddie

After buttoning up, she peddles away. Sometime later she finds something in the gutter. It's an aerosol paint can, and boy oh boy, is she excited! She shakes it up and begins painting a masterpiece on a nearby wall. *Here's a bear and here's a kitty and here's a snake and here's my mommy and . . . oops!*

She quits painting and turns around to face a big person. She sheepishly hands over the can, drops her head, and looks scared. *Yes, sir. No, Sir. Yes, Sir. I promise cross my heart!*

Home Again, Home Again!

The scolding finished, Molly races to the tricycle and peddles away. The bad feelings are quickly forgotten when the hunger sensation takes over. She hurries home, parks her tricycle, and walks inside to the kitchen. She says hello, sits down, waits for the plates of food to be served. After a quick saying of grace, she gulps down her milk, swallows her potatoes, but won't touch the spinach, not even at Mom's insistence. When Mom turns her back, Molly grabs the spinach and shoves it in her pocket. *See Mom, all gone. Yum!*

Excused from the table, she runs into her bedroom and pulls out a box of dolls from beneath her bed. She sits down on the floor and begins to play.

But little Molly is still too short for such a long day. Her eyes droop, the dolls fall, and sleep takes over. She curls into a snug little ball with a happy smile, dreaming about what the next day has to offer.

The Rope

The Line of Attention

Good friend Larry is in one big hurry today. *I've got to get this taken care of! I can't wait any longer!*

It's amazing that something on the ground is able to catch and hold his attention, but it does! He stops and looks at it. *What the heck is going on here? Oh, who cares! I've got things to do. I . . . I guess I can spare a few seconds. But ONLY a few!*

Larry lifts up the end of a rope. It stretches out before him, running off the side of the stage. Peer as he might, he can't see the end of it. He drops it and starts to walk away. *Rope. Big deal. What the . . . !*

The rope is sliding away from him! This intriguing rope has replaced whatever was uppermost in Larry's mind. He walks alongside it for a few steps, then decides to step on it to make it stop. Exercising more caution than previously, he picks it up and examines it. *You can't be too careful with these sliding ropes!*

Tug of War

Boop! The rope pulls itself out of Larry's hands and lands motionless on the ground. *What the heck is going on here, anyhowzits?*

He retrieves the rope, and again it tries to pull away from him. Larry is ready, though, and manages to hold on. The rope tugs again, more consistently and with greater power. Larry is jerked a few paces before he plants his feet and holds his position . . . and the rope.

The battle begins.

The rope pulls Larry, Larry pulls the rope. Back and forth across the stage they go, until poor Larry is near total exhaustion. But the rope throws in the towel first, releasing all pressure and falling slack, sending Larry tumbling backwards!

The Climb

Larry staggers to his feet, rope on the floor, and rubs his sore head. *Now why would a healthy rope all of a sudden decide to quit?*

Before he can straighten things out, the rope straightens itself out. Straight up! With the end dangling in front of his eyes, how can Larry help but try and pull it down? *Try* is about all he can do, too, for it won't budge. Larry looks up into the sky, searching for the end of the rope. *Wonder what the dickens is up there?*

Without hesitation (other than an obligatory spitting on the hands), Larry's climbing up the rope, pulling with his arms, shinnying with his legs. Before he knows it, he's at the top! *Now if I can just stand on the end of it, here . . .*

He makes it! Up so high, of course, the rope tends to sway, and Larry must work to maintain balance. He's quite pleased with the view, and points and smiles at a number of sights with which he is familiar. His sightseeing is cut short, however, by a sudden increase in the swaying of the rope. He slips off the end, but manages to grab the rope and slide down to the ground in safety. He wipes his brow and whistles. *Close call! Perfect except for the rope burns on the old paws!*

Toil to Coil

Let's get this thing wrapped up!

Larry pulls down on the rope and starts wrapping it in a coil. Suddenly it starts pulling against him and flies through the air, pivoting in his hands, as though it were a leash attached to a huge, soaring bird. The rope dips and dives and soars and spins tight little circles, long slow ones, and a few figure eights and Immelmann loops to boot! How *does* that Larry manage to hold on? He's dizzy, he's tired, he's . . . won! Larry beat the rope! It's on the floor, slack, just like a rope oughta be!

Two's Company

Larry smiles and looks down at two ropes. *What!?* That's right, *two* ropes.

Larry picks up both ends and examines them. Boop! One end begins pulling away! Boop! So does the other end! He's being stretched in half! Why doesn't he just let go?

Each rope begins yanking with incredible power. Larry jerks from side to side, hoping his arms won't be lost! *It's now or never, old chap!*

Knot Now!

He grits his teeth, scrunches his face, grimaces. Every muscle bulges. Slowly, very, very, slowly, the ropes move closer to-gether. Somehow, with a series of incredibly deft maneuvers, Larry manages to tie the two ropes together.

He steps back and admires his work: One taught line at chest level. *What to do now?*

That's easy to answer. He climbs onto the ropes and does a ropewalk act. He tiptoes his swaying body down the length, smiles, waves good-by, and disappears off the side of the stage.

Childbirth

Wake Up in There!

Tiny baby Carly lies curled in fetal position inside her mother's womb, her eyes shut tight. She shifts once or twice, but oh so slightly!

A moment later something seems to kick her! She jumps, but doesn't wake up. Another kick, another violent jump, and this time her eyes pop wide open. She struggles to sit upright with her arms and legs still curled close to the body. She looks around with genuine wonder—after all, this *is* the first time she's ever opened her eyes.

Playtime

Baby Carly stretches her arms out and presses against something soft and pliant. A little exploring reveals that she's wrapped in a giant, rubbery sack. With each push it stretches and loosens, until finally she can sit on her knees. She pushes up until she can stand. *This is more like it!*

Standing, she discovers the umbilical cord attached to her stomach. *What'll they think of next? Pretty nifty.*

She lifts it, twists it, and twirls it about, giggling and amazed at its versatility. *I wonder if I can . . . ?*

She sure can! She's a natural jump roper! What's this? After only a few jumps her world starts shaking. She falls down and tries to steady the rubbery walls. After all is safe she entertains a devilish thought. *That was kinda fun bouncing around like that!* She hauls off and plants a solid kick in the wall.

BOING! BOING! Baby Carly's having more fun than a kid in a carnival.

New Horizons

After getting her fill of cheap jollies, a sort of boredom sets in. She's jumped rope, kicked walls, stretched things around, and done her fare share of bouncing. What else is there to do?

She notices something in the wall in front of her. It's a hole! She reaches up and tries to pry it open. It's very tight and she can only open it a little bit, but it's enough to peer out through. Bright light pours in and she squints. She finds this a little frightening, but also very fascinating. Her strength can't hold out, though, and she lets go of the opening.

A Moment's Thought

Wow. What is all of that stuff out there?

She absently twirls her umbilical cord, not noticing the walls contracting against her. When she does notice, she's frightened. *It's tight in here! I can't move! I'm being squished!*

Desperately, she reaches for the opening, sticks her fingers in and begins to pry open. She struggles to get her hands out, then her arms, head, and torso. She gets one leg out and then pulls her foot (*got stuck somehow*) free. *Phew! That's hard work!*

Another View

Doctor Carly leans over the table and lifts a pair of scissors to make a quick cut, then ties a little knot. She lifts the newborn baby by the heels, gives it a slap on the bottom, turns it over, and hands it to someone else.

Looking down at the table, she sees something rather odd. She picks up the umbilical cord, one end in each hand, and twirls it as though it were a mini jump rope. *No! Couldn't be! I must be imagining things!*

Wally Says:

I like to use a real hockey stick in this routine. I guess I could use an imaginary one, but it's a lot more fun with the real thing! It's even more fun to use toothblack wax on my front teeth, yuk, yuk! If I was dumb enough, I could pass for a real goon! But I'm not! (I don't think . . .)

The Hockey Goon

Face Off!

Wally, infamous hockey goon of the great tundra, steps on the ice rink with his lips permanently sneered and eyes aglare. He's mad! *ARRRGH! Bite your face off, eh? Get it, face off?*

He slides to the center face-off ring and gets set. His skates are planted firm, he's crouched low, and his stick is on the ice in front of him. He looks up at his opponent and shakes a fist.

The ref drops the puck, and Wally only briefly chases it. He's more intent on lifting his stick into his opponent's crotch and smacking him in the face. That accomplished, he takes the puck away and smiles, showing his pearly whites. All two of them.

Cheated!

Wally skates more rapidly now, maneuvering the puck first this way, then that. He approaches the net, winds up, and lets go with a vicious slap shot—only to discover that he missed the puck. *ARRRGH!*

He looks down, makes a deft move with the blade, spins his body around, and makes a backhanded shot that sails into the net. HE SCORES! He lifts his arms and cheers.

The celebration is short-lived, however, for the goal isn't allowed. Wally argues with the ref, but with no results. He can't believe it! Snarling and muttering, he skates away.

Jawbusting as Playmaking

Back to the game!
Wally notices an opponent beside him and decides to fix the fellow up right by tripping him. Quick, simple. One quick last glance at the poor rookie before finding another victim. *Ha! What fun!*

But here comes the puck! He takes control, turns, passes to a teammate. He has more important things to do than play hockey.

Things like——smack a sucker over the head with his stick. Jab another in the face.

Here comes that darn puck again! He takes it, skates in a wide, fast arc. He turns backwards, looking, then forward again. An opponent comes and tries to steal the puck! *What do you think you're doing, jerko?* Wally laughs and smacks the upstart in the face. But when he looks down for the puck, it's gone! Looking back, he sees another player with it. He digs his blades in the ice and makes a sudden stop. No question about it, Wally is mad.

Picture of Innocence

In revenge, Wally skates behind another opponent and trips him, clobbers him with his stick, and then *jumps* on him! Up and down, up and down, smashing the poor guy to pulp. A ref blows the whistle and Wally stops. *Who, me? I wasn't doing anything to this guy, look . . .*

Wally picks the man up with one hand and points to him. The argument fails, Wally lets the pulp fall back to the ice, and heads to the penalty box. He opens the door, steps in and sits down.

Can't Keep a Good Man Down

Wally is a man of action, who, through years of sitting in the penalty box, has learned not to let it hamper his game. He cheers his team on, applauds them when they do something right, and slams the end of his stick down when they make a mistake. They seem to be making more mistakes than good plays, so Wally decides to help.

He casually and quietly slugs a passing skater in the head. Another skates by and Wally grabs him around the neck, shakes him, punches him, and gouges his eyes. *This is great! This is what hockey is all about!*

A third player skates by and Wally fails to grab him. Undaunted, he hurls his stick like a spear at the player. He watches it fly through the air . . . *Bingo! Meat for the table!*

Wally gets another stick and looks up at the clock. His penalty time is almost expired. He counts off on his fingers (to the best of his ability): *Three, five, two, NOW!*

He swings the gate open and races out to the action. A series of quick, agile skating moves, a few body checks, and Wally is skating full speed for the net with the puck.

A Kid at Heart

He shoots! It's blocked, rebounds! He shoots again, and again it's blocked! Frustrated, Wally slugs the goalie and watches him fall to the ice. He looks over his shoulder. *No penalty? Great!*

He flicks the puck into the unguarded net and scores! He throws his stick high in the air, hops up and down, and exchanges a few "high five" slaps with his teammates.

Skating away with a big smile on his face, he trips and falls down on his face. He touches his lip, sees a spot of blood, and starts to whimper, then cry. He looks again at the blood and cries even louder! He tries to get to his feet, but his skates keep slipping out from under him. In despair, he pounds his fists and feet on the ice.

Poor, misunderstood Wally. Everyone's always thought he was a mean, nasty hockey goon, while all along he had the heart (and stamina) of a young child.

Molly Says:

A fun prop to use in this routine is a sign that reads "Somewhere" on one side, and "Somewhere else" on the other side. I always get good laughs with that! If you don't like that, you can write the names of towns in the area in which you're performing: towns with funny names or funny reputations. Happy Traveling!

The Hitchiker

Thumbs Up!

Molly, a poor college student, resorts once again to hitchhiking to make it home for the holidays. She walks down the highway carrying a heavy backpack and stops at what she considers to be a favorable location. She labors to remove the backpack, drops it to the ground, sighs and rubs her sore shoulders. Reaching beneath her shirt, she pulls out a cardboard sign that reads "Somewhere" and sticks out her thumb.

Send in the Cars

Molly stands with an expectant smile on her face and looks for a car. *Nothing.* Even standing on her toes, she sees nothing. She purses and wiggles her lips: *Are all the cars participating in a giant parking marathon?*

But wait a minute! Here comes one now! Molly leans forward and holds her sign high and thumb out wide. *Puh-lease?* The car sails by. *There's plenty of fish in the sea!* She dismisses the car with a wave of her hand. Another one approaches and passes, as do many others. She begins to get angry. *I don't need to see all of the fish!* She shakes her fist at the next car that passes, only to be surprised when it stops. *Yahoo!* She picks up her heavy pack and lopes to the car as quickly as she can. When she reaches for the door handle, the car zooms away. Molly, exhausted and out of breath, collapses on her pack and tries to shake a weak fist.

After catching her breath, she again sticks out the old thumb. *What's this coming down the road?* She stands and starts to edge away from the road, a bit worried. A car is heading straight at her! Yikes! At the last instant she dives away and takes a tumble. *What are you trying to do? Kill me?*

Two's a Crowd

Molly's problems have only just begun. When she gets back to her spot, she sees another hitchhiker, waves, and exchanges a few brief words: *What? No, this is my spot. You move on down the road.* The other hitchhiker agrees and keeps on walking. When Molly is satisfied with the distance, she signals an okay sign.

Here comes another car! It slows and Molly smiles. *Oh boy, at last!* Unfortunately, the car rolls past Molly and stops for the other hitchhiker. *What about me? I was here first! That's not fair!*

Riding High and Wild

Moments later, another car swerves to an erratic stop beside Molly. She gets dizzy trying to follow its path! She bends over, studies the driver and frowns. The driver offers something to her. *A drink? No thanks. A ride? Well . . .*

Molly points to the sign that reads "Somewhere" and asks if

this is where the driver is going. *It is? Too bad.* She snaps her fingers and turns the sign around. It now reads "Somewhere Else." *This is where I'm going.* She waves good-by and watches the car lurch and weave away. *Phew! Close call!*

Out with the thumb and another car stops. She grabs her pack, throws it in the back door, and reaches for the front. Before she can grab the handle, the car speeds away! *That does it! I'm mad!* She picks up a few rocks and throws them at the car.

Another car stops and Molly carefully investigates. After deciding everything is all right, she gets inside, shakes hands with the driver, and permits herself a smile. Just as she stretches back to relax, the car stops. *What? You're turning here? But I only just got in!* She thanks the driver nonetheless and gets out.

Happier Trails

She turns and sees something in the bushes . . . her pack! *Hooray!* She picks it up and slings it over her shoulders. It may be heavy, but she's not letting go!

Another car stops. Extremely wary, she holds up her sign. *Is this where you're going? It is? Great!*

She runs to the car (offstage) and waves goodby to the audience. She's going home!

Larry Says:

Feel free to perform dual roles! Switch back and forth from the man to the dog. Kids will laugh when you pretend to be a dog. On the other hand, it's a real reward to meet the artistic demands of just playing the man, and leaving the dog to the imagination! Hey, try it both ways!

Walking the Dog

Law of the Leash

Larry is at home with a happy, eager look on his face. He reaches into a drawer and removes a leash, which he wraps in loose coils. Turning, he whistles, claps his hands, slaps his thighs, and calls for his dog, Spot. *Where the heck is that guy hiding, anyway?*

Larry bends over to peer beneath a table. He whistles, and Spot appears . . . from behind. The dog crashes into Larry and sends him sprawling. Spot's excited and gives Larry a few friendly licks, which Larry, fun guy that he is, returns. Larry gets to his feet and holds up the leash. *How about a little walk, eh, Spot old boy?*

Nothing doing! Spot promptly runs away and hides under the couch, much to Larry's disappointment. Larry tries to make light of it, laughing and chuckling. *C'mon, Spot, just a little walk?* Nothing doing.

Larry walks over to the couch, bends down and grabs for Spot. But Spot is quick. He evades the grab, and begins running around the room, with Larry close on his heels. In true rodeo fashion, Larry dives and tackles Spot, quickly wrapping the leash around his throat.

Stuck in Neutral

When he tries to pull Spot to the door, he finds the dog won't budge. Larry pulls on the leash with every ounce of strength. *Aaargh! Who glued my dog to the floor?*

Exhausted and frustrated, Larry walks behind Spot, looks over his shoulder to make sure no one is watching, and gives him a little kick in the tail. When nothing happens, Larry gets angry and winds up for a big kick. Before he can deliver it, though, Spot gets the idea and starts moving. Larry chuckles. *Just fooling, Spot. I wouldn't hurt you. Let's have that walk!*

Larry is now one happy guy, walking tall and proud. Spot seems to be having a good time, too, occasionally going faster than Larry and tugging on the leash. Larry waves to passersby.

Relief

Unexpectedly, Spot veers out to the side and stops. Larry is curious. *What's this all about, Spot old boy? Ah, er, right, yes, well . . .*

In imitation of the dog, Larry lifts one leg to his side and nods knowingly. Slightly embarrassed, he turns around and waits. And waits. Checks his watch. A quick glance over the shoulder: *Aren't you finished yet? Hurry it up!*

Larry continues to wait. He yawns and casually looks down at his feet. *Yuck!* He jumps to one side and sneers at Spot, then shakes his feet clean of Spot's . . . relief.

Fetch

After walking a while longer, Larry sees a stick and stops to pick it up. *Hey this could be real fun!*

He unleashes Spot and jumps up and down, waving the stick, trying to build a little excitement and enthusiasm for his plans. *Let's play catch!* He throws the stick and watches it land. *Go get it, Spot old boy!*

Spot won't move. He turns his head so that Larry has to walk around to face him. Larry stomps his foot and points to the stick. *Your master commands you to fetch!* Realizing that the situation is hopeless, Larry ties the leash back on Spot and drags him to the stick. He points at it. *Stick.* He puts it in his mouth, imitating what Spot should be doing, hops a few steps, drops the stick and wags his tongue. *Get the idea, Spot old boy?*

Of course not. Totally exasperated, Larry picks the stick up and tosses it away. *Out of sight, out of mind.*

This time, Spot decides he'll play fetch! Catching Larry off guard, he lunges madly for it, jerking Larry off his feet and onto his knees. Poor Larry is dragged along until Spot picks up the stick and offers it to his somewhat shaken master. Larry takes the stick, stands, and pats Spot on the head. *Good job. I'm proud of you. Also a little winded, if you don't mind!*

Wanting to end the game, he starts to toss the stick away, thinks better of it, and quietly tucks it away in his back pocket.

Contrary Canines Collide

Continuing on their merry way, Larry suddenly stops, stands on his tiptoes, and peers ahead. *Uh oh! Trouble!* He tries to steer Spot in another direction, but too late! Spot charges forward, dragging Larry behind. Panic City! As a last ditch effort, Larry jumps forward and picks Spot up in his arms.

The trouble turns out to be another dog. Larry yells at it, orders it to go away, and kicks at it. All to no avail, for the dog continues to jump for Spot, and Spot continues to escape Larry's clutches. It finally proves too much for Larry, who lets Spot slip away. He does, however, manage to hold on to the leash. Spot and the other dog run circles around Larry, who finally gives up. His head doesn't give up, though, and continues to follow the circular chase. Before Larry realizes it, he's being tied up by his own leash! He can't move. All he can do is wiggle his fingertips and strain his arms against the tight leash.

Spot manages to break free and run off with the other dog. *Get back here, Spot old boy. Spot! I mean it!*

Larry chases after Spot, hopping on two bound legs. *It's dog bones for dinner tonight, Spot! Your bones!*

Wally Says:

A fun costume to wear when performing this routine is a pair of suspenders and a wool cap. The color? Why, redneck red, what else?

In Search of the Perfect Tree

Lumberjack Wally, a none-too-bright backwoods yokel, walks through the country forest, breathing deeply the fresh, crisp air. His arms are filled with the tools he'll need for the day's work. He looks around now for a tree, finds one, and drops his tools so that he can investigate more closely.

He stands next to the tree and slaps it hard with his hand. *OUCH! Solid enough, all right, I reckon.* He arches his head back to look up to the top of the tree. It's high! He bends his head back further and further. His mouth gapes open. Wally finally bends back so far that he loses his balance and falls smack on his sitter! *Hmmph. Tree's big enough, all right, I reckon.*

He next measures the circumference of the tree. He stretches his arms out and reaches partway around the tree. Marking the spot where his right hand ends, he measures another arm's length. And another. *Wow! Fat enough, all right, I reckon!*

The Old-Fashioned Way

Wally brushes his hands clean and picks up his trusty ax. To test the sharpness of the blade, he pulls a hair. . . . *What the blazes?* Wally can't pull a hair from his head. Either his fingers are too weak, or, more likely, his hair is too greasy. Not one to be denied, he grabs a chunk of hair and hacks it off with the ax. From that chunk he removes a single strand and splits it lengthwise. *Sharp enough, all right, I reckon!*

He turns to the tree, positions himself, and starts chopping. Each time the ax hits, Wally's body shudders. On the third chop, a pine cone falls loose and hits him on the head. He lifts the cone, mutters, and tosses it away.

As if to get back at the tree for dropping the cone on his head, Wally swings the ax with increased power. The poor guy's body nearly shakes apart at the seams! He recovers and tries to pull the ax free from the tree. No luck, it's stuck! He pulls and twists and curses and kicks. Finally, he pulls on the handle with all his strength and it comes loose. Er, that is, the handle comes loose from the blade. Now Wally is in real trouble. . . .

Modern Times

Lumberjack Wally remembers! Not all is lost! He scurries to his pile of tools and pulls out a chainsaw! He starts after giving the usual fifty hard tugs on the starting rope, and begins to shake in harmony to the running motor. It's a wonder he can hold on to the saw, let alone try to cut with it. He smiles. *Horsepower enough, all right, I reckon.*

He goes to the opposite side of the tree and begins cutting. The blade kicks back a few times and almost causes the saw to twist free of his hands. Eventually, he manages to get a good cut going. This steadies the blade somewhat and decreases the vibrations. It also starts the splinters and chips flying, and Wally has to continually wipe clean his eyes and mouth and nose and ears.

Stuck Again!

Everything seems to be going hunky dory when all of a sudden, the chainsaw quits!

On closer examination, Wally sees that the saw is pinched tight in the tree. He mutters and tries to pull it free. *Ha! Solid as the sword in the stone, all right, I reckon!*

Bop! Another pine cone falls on his head. He looks up at the tree and shakes his fist.

Banging Away

Wally returns to the pile of tools and pulls out something very mysterious which he handles gently. He digs a small hole beneath the side of the tree and shoves in his surprise. Could it be dynamite? Yes! He connects a long fuse and pulls a lighter from his pocket. It won't light! Out of fuel!

Lumberjack Wally, however simple, is a determined man who will not be stopped. He must knock down that big tree. He is a man possessed. He is also a man of resources. Out of another pocket, he pulls a book of matches! The fuse is quickly lit and Wally runs for cover, plugging his ears.

K A B O O M !

The explosion sends Wally tumbling. He gets up, clears the dust clouds away, and walks back to the tree. It's still standing! This is too much! First the ax breaks, then the saw gets stuck, and now the dynamite fails. A defeated man, he puts an arm out and leans against the tree. While lamenting his fate, the tree starts to bend in the direction he's leaning! Wally notices his own body bending and puts two and two together: *Five! Falling fast, all right, I reckon.*

Pushme, Pullme

The tree stops. Wally pushes to help get it going again, but has no luck. *Hmm.* He leans against it to try and figure things out.

Before his slow mind can get a handle on the situation, it starts moving . . . back towards him! He gets frightened and starts pushing frantically against the tree. Further and further it bends, leaning over Wally at a menacing angle. He finally gives up and decides to run away. His sense of direction isn't too sharp, though, and he starts running *under* the length of the falling tree.

Realizing his predicament, he stops to figure things out. *If I take one step there, I'll be safe enough, all right, I reckon!* Smiling at his own flash of brilliance, he steps out of the danger zone. But what's this? He looks up and sees that the tree has altered its own direction, and is now above him. Wally again steps aside, and again the tree follows him! Again and Again! Yikes! It's falling! Here it comes!

Wally shuts his eyes and crosses his fingers.

A Job Well Done

The ground shakes and Wally's body rocks and trembles. A moment of silence follows. Carefully opening his eyes, Wally sees that he is safe. *Whew! Close call, all right, I reckon.*

He steps to the base of the tree, pulls out and opens a pocket-knife, and starts digging into the wood. He cuts out a little splinter and carefully carves it into a toothpick, with which he cleans his teeth. He grins, points to the toothpick and then to the fallen tree. *I carved me a toothpick, yuk, yuk!* He walks away cleaning his teeth.

Last Laughs

A pinecone falls on Wally's head. *Ouch!* He picks it up and tosses it at the tree that dropped it. But then another falls on him. *Ouch already!* And another pine cone! And another! HUNDREDS! Wally covers his head and runs for cover!

The Drunk

Happy Hour (in less than a minute)

Barfly Larry has had a bad day. He walks into the local watering hole with his hands in his pockets and his head hanging low. Life hasn't been treating him well. *I need a little "pick-me-up."*

He sits on the stool and leans against the bar, signaling for the bartender. *Gimme a double, eh, buddy?* A moment later, Larry nods his thanks and dumps some money on the bar. He holds his glass high and looks at it appreciatively. Like a ray of golden sunshine, it brings a smile to his face. With all due haste, he downs the contents in a single gulp.

ZINGO! The drink knocks Larry for a loop. He gasps for air and grabs the bar with both hands. His eyes bug wide and he shakes his head to clear away the effects. *Hot dog! Bartender, bring me the whole bottle.*

Larry takes the bottle and quickly refills his glass.

New Friends for Old

Although Larry doesn't gulp his second and third drinks, he does consume them at a fairly rapid pace. He looks down at the end of the bar and sees someone he knows. He waves and picks up his drink to join the other man. The effects of three quick drinks are already apparent in Larry's walk and gestures. Larry pats his friend on the back, exchanges greetings, and leans against the bar to order another drink.

Larry starts talking. Continues talking. His mouth is relentless! What was once a depressed fellow is now a gleeful gabber. He gestures flamboyantly and hits the head of the man sitting next to him at the bar. Larry turns and apologizes profusely. Apparently having completely forgotten about his previous companion, Larry offers to buy a drink for the man he hit on the head. After the bartender fills their glasses, Larry makes a lunge and grabs the bottle out of his hands. *I'll save you the running around, pal, how about it? Har, har, har!*

Larry begins conversing with his new buddy as though they were old childhood friends, drinking freely and becoming more and more intoxicated. He leans into the fellow and begins lectur-

ing on something most terribly important, adding emphasis with repeated fingerpoking into the man's chest.

An accidental clunk on the head is one thing, intentional jabbing is another. Much to Larry's surprise, the man walks away. *Hey, buddy? Hey, what about your drink? Hey, dontcha want it? Okay.* Not being one to let things go to waste, Larry drinks it for him.

Bottle Stalking

Larry's frivolity is not lessened by his loneliness. With a mechanical laugh, he settles down for some serious drinking. He grabs for the bottle, but misses. *Hey? What kind of game is this?* A bit of meanness begins to emerge.

Holding one unsteady finger between his eyes and the bottle, he tries to focus. Seeing what appears to be two bottles, he holds up a second finger and giggles. *This could be a problem.*

He puts both arms on the bar and begins to surround the elusive bottle (or bottles, depending on your view). *Gotcha!* He grabs the bottle with both hands and takes a long, sloppy swig. He wipes his face off and stands (however unsteady).

The Incredible Journey

A new awareness enters Larry's psyche. He brings his knees close together and frowns. The alcohol that traveled through his mouth to his brain has now traveled to his bladder. *I gotta go potty.*

With bottle in hand, Larry sets out on his trek. He stumbles and veers and waves his arms about for balance. He occasionally grabs onto something or someone, and immediately thanks the person (or thing). If he didn't have to go to the bathroom so badly, he'd stop and chat (though what would he say to a pool table?). But with his legs clamped tight together and his body bent at the waist, Larry merely points to the bottle and then to the bathroom. A simple, but honest, excuse.

At long last he approaches the door. He holds his arms out wide and shouts. *Eureka!* He grabs the handle and tries to turn it, but . . . can it be? It won't turn! It's locked! Larry is frantic! He clenches his legs and wraps his arms around his waist, grimacing and fretting. He's in so much pain, he takes another swig from his bottle.

I can't take it any longer! Hurry up in there!

Larry begins pounding on the door. Bam! Bam! Bam! Ba— . . . oops. His arm stops in mid-air when the door opens. *Er, gee, I didn't er . . .* Larry sheepishly steps aside to let the man out, then dives in.

One for the Road

After finishing his lengthy visit, Larry steps back into the bar. He's still drunk, but is no longer intrigued by his surroundings. Looking at his watch (and asking someone else to decipher it for him), he sees that it's time to leave.

He waves to his assumed friends and *oh, what the heck, one more for the road.* He steps up to the bar and swallows a drink in one gulp. *Whew! They sure don't make it like that anymore!* He sets the glass down, waves good-bye, and walks outside to his car.

Things That Go Bump in the Night

He fumbles in his pocket for his keys, pulls them out, and drops them. Getting down on his knees he giggles, finds them, and tries (several times) to get the door key into the lock. When he succeeds, he opens the door and crawls in.

He starts the car, puts it in gear, and jerks and chugs away. Larry has to struggle to control the car, but he doesn't mind. In fact, he thinks it's fun! He spins the wheel back and forth, steps on the throttle for exhilarating bursts of speed, and beeps his horn. *Whoopee!*

Drowsiness soon gets the better of laughing Larry. Try as he might, he can't fight off shutting his eyelids for just a few seconds. When they slide back open . . . *Lookout Larry old buddy old boy!* He slams on his horn and jumps on his brakes. Too late! He hits something and his body twists and flies. Remarkably, he's unhurt. Understandably, he's angry. *Why can't things be more careful and stay out of my way?*

Hangover Supreme

Larry stumbles out of the car to investigate, shouting and waving his fists. He's surprised, then frightened, to find someone (*a real human!*) sprawled in front of the car. He grabs the victim by the shoulders and begins shaking. *Wake up! Wake up! Don't do this to me!*

Larry smiles. *That's better! You were beginning to fool me there for a minute!* The victim slowly gets to his feet. Larry puts his arm around the person and pulls a few dollars out of his billfold. *Here, take this and keep it quiet, huh?*

The victim refuses. Instead, the victim slugs Larry and knocks him over. Larry gets up and shakes a fist at the exiting victim. *That's gratitude for you!* He gets into his car and reaches for the keys. For the first time, he pauses and thinks, somewhat soberly. A long glance towards the victim. He sighs, pulls the key out of the ignition, and tosses them out of the window.

I'm not that drunk, mind you, but I am kind of sleepy. Besides, what's the hurry?

Larry curls up and goes to sleep, like all good drunks should.

Wally Says:

If you're a closet schizo like yours truly, you'll enjoy switching back and forth from the role of Welterweight Wally to Heavyweight Harold. How to change personalities in the middle of a routine? Just turn around slowly and presto! Easier than changing underwear. Might I also suggest a plastic mouthpiece and small stool as props?

The Boxer

In This Corner, Welterweight Wally

Wally, a meek little guy, stands before the ring, knocks his gloves together, and bounces on his toes. He's ready for action! He climbs through the ropes and into the ring, keeping his gloves in motion and loosening up for the big fight.

He goes to his corner, grabs the ropes, and keeps his feet dancing. Off comes his robe, in goes the plastic mouthpiece! His gloves are raised high in the air. *I am the Champion!*

Stepping into the center of the ring, Wally lets the master of ceremonies raise his arm and announce him to the crowd. His bow consists of a nod of the head and touching his brow with his glove. After his arm is dropped, Heavyweight Harold is introduced.

And in This Corner, Heavyweight Harold

Harold is one big muscle that has never smiled. Mean is his middle name. He raises his arm and looks down on puny little Wally. He scoffs with amusement. *Me? Against this little runt? Who's putting me on?*

Wally's Woeful Wonderings

Wally quits bouncing on his feet. To take in all of Harold's height, he has to crane his head back. *Wow. Big. Mean. Trouble.* He's so awed he absently spits out his plastic mouthpiece. After scurrying to pick it up, Wally looks back at Harold and decides a tiny little mouthpiece isn't going to do him much good. He tosses it away.

A shudder runs through him and he returns to his corner, sitting on a chair. The bell rings and Wally jumps up as though it were inside his head.

Harold Sets the Pace

Harold leaves his corner and stomps forward. He pauses to flex the muscles in his arms and back. He's ready to fight. He puts his dukes up and begins moving in a lumbering sort of circle. (You couldn't honestly say Harold *dances*.)

Wally Meets His Match

Wally puts his own dukes up (or is he covering his eyes?) and hopes for a mercifully short bout. He charges forward ... BONG! Harold immediately clobbers him on the head. Wally bounces into the ropes and back out, receiving another clobber. This painful process is repeated several times, ending only when he falls to his knees. With his eyes crossed and his tongue dangling, he makes the mistake of grabbing the ropes and pulling himself back to his feet.

Harold's Heyday

Harold has never had so much fun in his life. He almost smiles as he picks up poor Wally by the head and slings him, like a rag doll, onto the floor. Whap! Whap! Whap!

To vary the pace, he twirls Wally around like he was a rope, and tosses him high into the air. Wally lands on Harold's fist and slumps to the ground.

Time Out for Wally

Wally staggers to his feet and holds up his arms. *Wait a minute, Harold, let me save you the trouble.* Nice guy that he is, Wally hits himself on the head. Ouch! As he's a bout to repeat, the bell rings and ends the round. *Whew!* Wally wipes his brow with relief and grabs onto the ropes so he can find the way to his corner.

He's bushed, plain and simple. He pulls his chair out to sit down—misses it and plops on the floor. He's too tired to care. *What am I doing here?* While deep in thought, he takes out a comb and tidies his hair. *This is a rough fight. What am I going to do?*

The bell rings to start the second round and Wally drags himself to his feet. This time, what the heck, he throws all caution to the wind and charges forward with his teeth gritted and anger and determination written boldly on his face. He meets Harold and begins landing powerful, vicious blows. After a dozen or so swings, he steps back to appraise the damage. *Hmm. Nothing.*

Undaunted, he resumes his attack.

Harold Lifts a Finger

Harold looks down on Wally and actually laughs! *What is this pipsqueak doing to me? That tickles! Hey, cut it out!*

His patience is shortlived. Harold cuts short the lesson in tickling by lifting one fist and slamming down on the top of Wally's head.

Whirling Wally

Wally reels as he's hit, stumbling back into his seat. In a daze, he leans outside the ropes, grabs a little hammer, and hits the bell. His head shakes and he recovers his senses.

Combing his hair, he plots out a new strategy. *Of course! That'll work! It has to!* A quick touch-up with the can of hair spray, and he's back in the fight!

He begins his new strategy not by exchanging blows with Harold, but by slowly circling him and displaying some fancy footwork. Harold takes a few swings, but Wally is quick enough to dodge them. He moves faster and faster, until he's eventually running tight, rapid circles around Harold, not to mention making funny faces and taunting gestures!

Harold Halts

Big Harold looks like a fool trying to follow Wally around the ring. Before he knows it, he's dizzy as a drain! He falls to the floor and tries to get up, but his sense of balance evades him. He can't get up.

Wally Wins!

Wally stands over Harold and counts to ten! He's won! He dances a little jig and throws his hands in the air. The Champion! Again he throws his hands up and—BOP! He accidentally clips himself on the chin and begins to stagger, then slowly falls down on his face.

He smiles: *Two KO's in one fight! Incredible!*

Carla Says:

This is a fun routine, and it's easy to add your own little touches to it. All you've got to do is repeat what you do every morning. Better yet, take a nap on stage before show time, and set your clock for the opening curtain. That's what I do for a natural, unforced performance.

Late for Work

Nighty-night!

Cozy Carla yawns and stretches out to the ends of her toes. It's late and she is one very sleepy lady.

Her eyelids droop and fall shut. Slowly, her heads tilts to one side and she begins breathing deeply. Carla's falling asleep on her feet! Only in the nick of time does she shake herself awake to prevent crashing to the floor. *Tee hee! Silly me! Must be time for beddy-bye!*

She half walks, half stumbles to bed, where she takes her clothes off. The shirt unbuttons easy enough, followed by the unbuckling of the belt, the kicking off of the shoes, and the dropping of the pants. *Hey? What's going on here? Did my feet grow?*

Her pants are stuck on one foot and all the pulling in the world won't get them off. Frustrated, she kicks wildly, causing the pants to go flying off to a far distant corner. *Where they land, nobody knows!*

Don't Let the Bedbugs Bite!

Carla leans over the bed and carefully peels back the covers. She yawns and rubs her eyes. *Ah, bed.* She fluffs the pillow and starts to climb in. *Yick! Eek! What's this?*

She lifts the covers and, using the tips of her forefinger and thumb, pulls something small out and drops it on the floor, quickly stomping it with her bare feet. *Oops! Shouldn't have got carried away.*

Carla shudders and scrapes her foot clean on the floor. Whatever was on her foot must have been yuk, yuk, yukky!

Jingle Jangle

She finally makes it into bed, pulls the covers tight, and sets the clock. After winding it tight, she quickly falls to sleep.

Night passes, all in the space of five or six long, deep, snoring breaths.

The alarm goes off, and Carla jumps up to a sitting position, dazed. Her head bounces and jangles to the rhythm of the alarm. She puts her hands over her ears to stop the noise and succeeds. *No more noise! No more headbouncing!*

Even though she's still half asleep, she finds this amusing. She takes one hand away to reach for the clock, but her head starts bouncing so much she quickly returns the hand. She can't help but laugh! Experimenting, she pulls her hands off her ears and replaces them, quickly, several times in succession. Each time her head bounces. *Okay, fun is fun, but I've got to get some more sleep!*

She grabs the clock, head and body bouncing, and tries to turn off the alarm. No such luck. What else can she do but throw it across the room? CRASH! Her head quits bouncing as she returns it to the pillow.

Later That Day . . .

She finally stirs herself awake. She smiles and stretches, fully rested. Absently reaching for her clock, she can't find it and becomes somewhat puzzled. *Where could it be? Ah, I know!*

She reaches down beneath the covers, way down to her toes, and smiles. *The clock.* The smile vanishes. She pulls out another one of those *yukky things*, tosses it on the floor, and jumps out of bed to stomp on it. *Oh, not again!* Yes, again she did her stomping with bare feet. Shaking her head, she sees something out of the corner of her eye. The clock!

She quickly runs to it, picks it up, and looks at the time. *Oh my! Oh dear! Oh oh! Late for work!* She throws the clock in the air and claps her hands on her face.

Hurryin' and Scurryin'

If there's one thing Carla knows, it's how to make up for lost time. Her actions are now fast and furious, even if it means doing a few things backwards.

She rushes into the bathroom and turns on both faucets in the sink. After washing her face and hands, she wipes them dry with a towel and pauses to look at herself in the mirror. *Yick! Is that me? Where did all these wrinkles come from? Why is my face falling? Gee . . . hey, I'm late!*

She picks up the toothbrush and toothpaste and rolls her tongue across her teeth. *I hope it hasn't taken root, yet. Yuk!* She tries to squeeze paste out of the tube and nothing emerges. She squeezes harder, and still nothing. Hold on. Something did come out, but at the wrong end. She scrapes the paste onto her brush, gives her teeth a quick going over, and gargles with a glassful of

water. Before she spits it out, however, she swallows it! *Now what the heck did I do that for?*

Now for the hair. She grabs a comb and is able to control all but one stubborn hair that wants to stick straight up. In desperation she squirts a little toothpaste onto the comb and gets the hair to comply.

Tummy Time

Carla heads for the kitchen, rubbing her tummy and licking her lips. *I can't think until I get rid of this growling.*

She takes two eggs out of the refrigerator and, just for the heck of it, juggles them a time or two. One too many, at any rate, for she drops one and has to get another. She sets a pan on the stove, turns on the heat, and cracks open the eggs. *Now where am I going to put these shells? I know!* Over her shoulder.

She takes a bag of bread, pulls out two slices, and drops them in the toaster. From a cupboard above, she finds a plate and fork and sets them on the counter. *Be right back!*

Attire Retired

Now for some clothes.

Carla runs to the bedroom, picks up her shirt, buttons it, then finds her pants. *How'd they end up over here, anyway?* She starts to put them on, then stops and sniffs. Something is . . . burning! She drops the pants on the floor and flies back to the kitchen.

It's the toaster! She flips a button and the toast flies in the air. Making a grab for it, she discovers it's very hot and tosses it aside, blowing her fingers.

But again she smells something. The eggs! She turns the heat off, grabs the pan, and flips the eggs onto her plate. *Ah, time to eat!* Her smiling face turns into a sneer when she finds the eggs are so hard she can't cut them. *I don't care! I'm late! I'm hungry!*

She grabs the eggs with her hands and opens her mouth! In they go! *YOW! HOT!* Out they go! Her eyes follow the path of the hard, bouncing eggs until they are out of sight. *I'd hate to see the chickens that laid those!*

Giving up on eating (while she's ahead), Carla quickly puts on a pair of shoes and takes a deep breath. *Ready for work!*

Look Out World!

Carla hurries out the front door, runs down the porch stairs, and down the street. *Where's that bus?* She waits impatiently until it arrives, then smiles as it pulls to a stop. She climbs on board and begins to look for a seat until the driver stops her. She rubs her finger and thumb together. *Money? Oh, ha ha, silly me. Sure, no problem. I'll just reach in my pocket and . . . my pocket and . . . MY POCKET!*

Sure enough, she forgot to put on her pants! She tries covering herself while backing out of the bus. *Wait here! Just be a sec.* Zip! Back down the street, back up the stairs, back in the bedroom, pants on, and all the way back to the bus with money in hand. Hey, wait!

Carla is left standing, coughing in the fumes of the departing bus. She trudges back home and sits on her bed, dejected. That familiar drowsiness returns, however, and she finds herself crawling back under the covers. It's been a rough and tumble day. *YIKES! Not again!* She reaches under the covers and pulls out another one of those yukky things. *Gimme a break, huh?*

Molly Says:

Get heavy! This routine is even more dramatic if you have some sound effects: Specifically, an assistant (offstage) with a loud, clear percussion instrument (two blocks of wood work great) keeping a steady even beat similar to a heartbeat or ticking of a clock. Also, keep your feet moving so it looks like you are walking forward (or, should I say, so it looks like you are standing still while the world passes you by?).

The Journey

Planning Stages

Gestating Molly lies curled in a fetal position inside the womb, just waiting. A single, soft tick of a clock (or heartbeat) sounds and her head lifts. The tick sounds again, but louder. Molly gets to her knees. Another tick and her eyes open. She reaches forward and crawls out of the womb. The ticking now assumes a full, regular beat.

A Journey of a Thousand Miles Begins With . . .

Molly is on her knees, a toddling baby, crawling forward in time with the ticking. She reaches up to mommy and nurses for a moment. She finishes, licks her lips, and something new comes to her attention—her feet.

She tremulously lifts one leg and plants it firm. Then the other. A little precarious and wobbly, but she's learning to walk . . . forward, towards something in the distance.

Kids!

Here come children her own age! Oh boy! She waves and joins in a game of jumprope. Things go alright for a moment, but she trips and drops the rope. Not having time to stop walking forward, she leaves it behind and waves goodbye.

Molly waves to another playmate. They quickly get into an argument and Molly hits her. To her surprise, a Big Person grabs her and gives her a few swats on the bottom. Molly cries, but the tears dry soon enough.

School

A teacher shoves a book into her hands. She opens it, turns the pages, and mouths the words. Soon she's reading silently and thoughtfully, turning the pages faster and faster, taking notes and making calculations. Molly is surprised when the book is ripped out of her arms. Continuing to walk forward, she looks over her shoulder to see who took it.

Disturbing Growth(s)

Before she can figure out who took her book, she notices some changes in her own body. Molly, always walking forward, waves to new friends, talks rapidly (and a bit absently?), and tries on makeup. She picks up a pair of pom-poms and leads the cheer at the big game. Hooray! She throws the pom-poms up in the air: They sail away behind her. She looks back at them and bumps into someone.

Picking Partners

At first she's embarrassed. However, she's quickly attracted to the man she bumped into. She starts walking with a little extra swing in the hips, smiles, talks with him, and teases. A quick kiss on the cheek. Marriage? She gulps and her eyes go wide. She nods slowly: Yes.

She walks down the aisle holding her bouquet, lifts her veil, and kisses her husband slowly and solemnly.

Nervously, she peels her clothes off so that they can make love. She embraces him and is quickly lost in the throngs of passion. When it is over, the husband pulls away and Molly pulls away, waving good-by. She is happy, content.

Footstep Follower

Surprise! She's pregnant and her stomach is swelling! It gets bigger and bigger and—a moment of pain, clenched teeth, and she gives birth. She takes the babe in her arms and rocks him back and forth. She nurses him. When the child is too big and heavy to hold, she puts him on the ground and walks hand in hand. The child grows until he is as tall as she, then takes his own path. She waves goodbye.

The Golden Gray Years

Molly walks a little slower and rubs at some pains in her back and finger joints. She picks up a book to read and finds she needs a pair of glasses. She tries reading, can't figure it out, shakes her head and drops the book.

Brushing her hair, she finds a few gray hairs and hastily pulls them out. But there are more! Too darn many to bother pulling! Oh, let them go . . .

Walking now with a distinct curve in her back, she develops a slight limp and has to make use of a walking cane. She waves to people and tries to talk, but no one is interested in what she has to say. Molly dismisses these rude people with a wave of her hand.

Tick Tock, Knock Knock

Molly thinks she sees something in the far distance, but isn't sure. She walks a little faster, and the ticking sound grows more rapid, louder. What does she see?

The ticking suddenly gets much louder, much faster, and Molly moves slower. A pause . . . silence, silence . . . Molly takes a final step, drops her cane, reaches out for something. . . . The final tick is loud, abrupt.

Molly grabs at her heart and stands motionless with a sad smile on her face. The lights fade very slowly to black.

Carla Says:

For an excellent practice session, put in a long day of kite flying! It's been too long since you've last flown one, anyway!

High as a Kite

Thrills and Dreams

Carefree Carla runs to the park carrying her yet to be assembled kite. She's as excited and happy as any young woman could possibly be. So excited, in fact, that she trips flat on her face and bites her tongue. *Ouch! I didn't swallow it, did I? No. Good!*

Deciding that where she had fallen is a perfectly good spot, she begins to unravel the kite for assembly. She ties the two sticks into a cross shape, then attaches the paper. Putting a bend in the frame, she ties a string across the back, then holds it high. As she looks at the kite, a dreamy smile crosses her face, and her eyes shut. She holds her arms out like a bird and sways . . . *I'm flying, flying, over the clouds and rivers and . . .*

Back to Basics

But enough! Back to the business at hand!

Carla studies the kite and decides something is missing . . . *but what, what, WHAT!?*

A scratch on the head brings the answer. The tail is missing! And poor Carla has nothing to use for a tail. Unless . . . but no! She couldn't do that. Just couldn't. Or could she? Why yes, come to think of it, she can and will do *that!* In a flash, before she can change her mind, she peels off her shirt and tears it into strips. She ties them together to form a tail and hooks it to the kite.

Not a bad idea! I do wish it were a little warmer, though. Brrrr!

Next, she ties the string to the kite and bites off the loose end. The bit of string becomes wedged in her teeth and she must carefully pull it out. She has to pull very hard, and when it finally comes free, she almost falls over. A bit dazed, she wiggles her jaw and checks for missing teeth.

Up, Up and Away!

Carla decides it's time to fly. She picks up the kite and string, which is wound around a stick. With a mighty throw, she hurls the kite into the air! Plop! She tries again and meets the same success. Muttering unrepeatables, she changes strategies.

This time, she picks up the kite and runs with it, carefully unravelling a bit of string from the stick. It begins to rise! She stops to admire her minor achievement, only to watch it wriggle (as only kites can do) slowly to the ground. Undaunted, the spunky kiter tries again. This time when she stops, she occasionally tugs on the string to maintain lift. Still, it moves slowly to the ground. Carla tugs frantically, and, at the very last minute, it works its way up! *Yahoo! It's working! It's flying!*

Carla has to gulp air to catch her breath, she's so darn excited!

Obstacle Course

Carla continues to raise the altitude of the kite, by unwinding string from the stick. Suddenly, the kite starts to veer to the left! With some careful, albeit frantic, maneuvering, Carla manages to get it back where she wants it . . . and then some!

Now it's moving to the right, towards the big jagged trees that grab kites. She tries signalling this information to the kite. *Oh, now I'm going crazy. That kite can't hear me!* She tugs the string and runs to her left, but doesn't seem to be able to stop the kite from moving the wrong way!

Unable to watch it's imminent demise, Carla covers her eyes with her free hand. *Of course, I've just got to have a little, tiny, peek!*

What do you know! The kite changes direction in the nick of time! Saved!

A Good Way to Unwind

The kite flies higher and higher, and all the while, Carla has a grand time. This is what kite flying is all about: smooth sailing on a sunny day. The dreamy smile finds its way to Carla's face once again, and her eyelids start to droop shut. Meanwhile, she absently continues to unwind the string.

Surprise! Her smile vanishes and her hand freezes! She looks down. *The string! It's gone! All I've got is a stupid stick!*

She finds the string ahead of her, dragging on the ground. She chases after it, making several grabs, each time coming up empty-handed. Finally, out of desperation, she makes one big headlong lunge and falls to the ground. A moment of silence and stillness. Slowly, she lifts her head and looks. At the tip of her outstretched finger at the end of her outstretched arm is the very end of the string. She quickly grabs it and ties it to the stick, then

has to do some fast and furious work to get the kite back up to its proper elevation.

Whew! I didn't know kite flying could be so exciting!

Temptations Along the Path

After a moment of solitary flying, a young, handsome man approaches. Carla (to herself), raises her eyebrows, smiles, and indicates (by outlining with her hands) that the man has a good build. She calls to him. He stops and they talk, laugh, giggle, and blush. Feeling confident, Carla moves beside him to put her arm around his waist, but the man stops her.

What's that? Only if I let you fly my kite? You're joking! You're not? Why, you disgusting, ugly, conniving . . . !

She dismisses the man with a wave of her hand. She's sorry, but kite flying is a very personal thing to her. She pats her heart and points to the kite.

Winds O' Call

She returns her attentions to the kite. A few corrective tugs and the kite is back in proper position. Carla is in heaven, now, right beside the kite! She holds her arms out like wings and sways. What a wonderful life!

Unaware of what's happening, a strong wind begins to blow against her back. She leans back into it, naturally, taking short steps forward. A big gust almost knocks her over. *What the heck is going on? Is this a tornado or something?*

She hurriedly tries winding the kite back in. But after a few turns she stops and reconsiders. Even while fighting a mean wind, a smile comes to her face and she lets the string go, tossing aside the stick. *So long, friend.*

With that high as a kite smile, she turns into the wind and holds her arms out like wings, pretending to fly. Or is she pretending? She looks down . . . *YIKES! What am I doing up here?* She starts flapping her arms (wings?) furiously and floats away.

Molly Says:

This is a classic! Try your own variation. Don't let my instructions box you in! Get it? "Box" you in? You do? What's that? Shut up and start the routine? I was going to get "around" to it! Get it, "arou—" . . . oh, all right!

The Box

Boxed In

Molly sits on the floor with her head hanging down, fast asleep. With a decisive *snap!* she sits upright, opens her eyes, yawns and stretches her arms out—*Hey! Who's crowding my space?*

It seems as though there are two walls, one on each side, which prevent her from stretching. Not terribly bothered, she turns slightly and tries stretching her arms to the front and back. Fat chance! There are walls there, too!

Molly can't help but be a little disconcerted, if not irritated. At least she can still lift her arms and—a ceiling! No more than a foot above her head! *That does it! I'm boxed in!*

Roominations

Molly puts her elbows on her knees and her chin in her hands, then taps a temple with her fingers. She decides it's time for a closer examination of the situation.

Running her hands along the floor, she defines a right angle where it meets the front wall. Then she finds the front corners and slides her hands up to the top corners, checking the ceiling. Everything is tight, smooth and neat. The walls and ceiling are solid: They won't be budged.

The heck they won't!

Expanding One's Parameters

Determined to work her way out, Molly leans against a side wall and pushes against it with her hands and shoulders.
Rrrrrrgh! Ooooomph!
Nothing.

She relaxes and droops her shoulders in despair. A fierce desperation overtakes her, however, and she lunges wildly and frantically into the wall. *Out! Let me out of here! I'm cracking, I'm . . .*

Still, nothing. She drops her head and quietly begins to cry. Resigned to defeat, she leans against a wall. Slowly, slowly, the wall (unbeknownst to Molly) begins to *slide* away! Poor Molly finally hits the floor with a slightly painful clunk and stops crying. *Either that wall moved or I shrunk!*

If one wall can move, then . . .

She pushes against the opposite wall. It slowly eases out, as do the front and back walls when they are pushed. She can stretch out (*boy, does that feel good!*) but still can't stand up.

Up and At 'Em

Molly puts both hands on the ceiling, grits her teeth and pushes. Nothing moves.

Let's try something else.

Molly decides to work on the edge of the ceiling. She moves to one side and gets on her knees so she can use a little more muscle. This time the ceiling moves, up and up, until finally she is standing with her arms stretched high. Quite pleased with herself, she turns and bumps into an unpleasant surprise. Only one side of the ceiling went up, having pivoted on the opposite wall. *Sorry, I'm not into slanted ceilings.*

With a few grunts and grimaces, Molly lifts the other side of the ceiling. She can now stand in a room with two or three steps of breathing space. *Not bad, but she'd really rather be on the outside looking in.*

Hold On, Holed Out

Molly catches something out of the corner of her eye. Bending for a closer examination, she finds that where a wall meets the floor she can very barely stick her little finger through a teensy weensy hole.

With a great effort, she *lifts* up on the wall and raises it a foot or two. It's hard work, but she's excited. She lifts a little higher and puts both hands under the bottom edge of the wall. When it's above her head, she steps out of the box and lets the wall fall. Unfortunately, she doesn't move her hands fast enough. *Ouch! I'm stuck!*

She slides her hands out with agonizing pain and holds them up (with the backs facing the audience). Her fingers are missing! She gulps. *What am I going to do?*

As though she knew all along what she was going to do, she sticks a thumb in her mouth and blows. Poof! The fingers pop up, fully restored.

The Little Squeeze

Molly decides that something has to be done about the box. She moves to the back wall and pushes it in, putting it back to its original position. She does the same with the side and front walls.

The ceiling is a different matter. It's a little too tall for her to get a good grasp on, so she tries a different tack. She leans against the side and tries to push the structure over, onto the floor. It tilts, then reverses directions and aims for Molly. She dodges out of the way in the nick of time!

CRASH!

Molly smiles and goes to the top of the box (or what was once the top!) and pushes in. Now the box is big enough for her to put her arms around, which she does. She squeezes it smaller and smaller. Finally, she has nothing but a very small cube, She smiles, flicks it up in the air, and catches it in her back pocket.

Nothing to it!

Her problems solved, she skips away. SMACK!

What's this? Another wall? Oh, dear, it can't be!

She turns around and bumps into another wall. Walls in front and behind, too!

Aaargh! There oughta be a law!

Wally Says:

Be careful to keep your actions sharp and precise, just like a machine! And be glad you're a professional mime (aren't you?) so you don't have to be a widget worker! Remember, the success of this routine depends mostly on your display of technical skills, so make 'em good.

The Widget

First Day on the Job

Wally, a Blue Collar Worker, springs lightly down the street, looking for his new place of work. He stops in front of a building and pulls a card out of his pocket to check the address. *You betcha! Addresses match. This is the place!*

He steps forward and climbs a short flight of stairs. After a brief pause to tidy his clothes and hair, he reaches to open the door. He steps inside the building and finds a busy place. His head can't turn fast enough to catch sight of all the action. *Hey! Can somebody help me? I gotta job here!*

Wally changes to FRITZ THE FOREMAN.

Introductions

Fritz is a big, mean, strong foreman. He barks out a few orders to his workers and sees Wally. Angrily chomping on a cigar, he acknowledges the new kid. With his hands on his hips he stalks over to Wally and sizes him up: *Yeah? Whaddya want?*

Fritz changes to WALLY.

Wally is a little intimidated by Fritz's behavior, but still manages to smile and extend a friendly handshake. Refused, Wally meekly pulls his hand back and pulls out some papers. *See, sir?*

I'm supposed to work here? That's right, that's my name.
Wally changes to FRITZ.

On the Job Training

Fritz takes the papers, reads them and laughs. *You! Work here? Ha! That'll be fun to see!. Ha!*

Fritz motions for Wally to follow. He leads him to a spot on the assembly line and shows him the ropes.

Number One. Lift raw materials from basket on floor and reach up high to dump them into Chute A.

Number Two. Materials fall onto Assembly Belt B.

Number Three. When materials get to here, push Button C with the left hand.

Number Four. Turn Dial D with the right hand.

Number Five. Quickly punch Buttons E, F, G with the left hand.

Number Six. Kick lever H with right foot.

Number Seven. Flip Switches I, J, K with right hand.

Presto! Widget is complete and finished!

Fritz lifts it and show Wally how long and sleek it is: *something a guy can be proud of, y'know?* He then puts it back on the belt so it can be transported elsewhere.

Fritz jabs his finger at Wally: *You understand what to do? Good!* Fritz changes to WALLY.

Wally Tries

Before Wally can answer, Fritz turns away to attend to other matters. *Hey, wait a minute! I'm not sure I do understand what . . .* But Fritz is long gone.

Wally turns to face the complex manufacturing machine and scratches his head. *Let's see . . . this goes here, and . . . hmm, no, that goes . . . oh well, I'll figure it out!*

He lifts an armful of materials and dumps them into Chute A. *Is that enough? Maybe a few more . . . Woops! Too much! Aw, the heck with it! It'll work fine.*

Wally turns and readies himself. When the parts come out of Chute A and onto Belt B, he starts to push Button C, but hesitates. *Can't be right.* Instead, he pushes Buttons E, F, and G. Next, he flips Switches I, J, and K. He kicks Lever H (OUCH!) and gives Dial D a quick spin. *Nothing to it!*

But when the Widget comes out, Wally grimaces. *Yick!* He

picks it up and tries to polish it with his sleeve. *Hmm.* Turning, he sees Fritz coming and quickly hides the Widget under his shirt.

Wally changes to FRITZ.

Not a Government Job

Fritz is genuinely angry. He looks around for the Widgets and is amazed that there are none. He sees something under Wally's shirt and quickly grabs it. *A mangled Widget! You airhead! You ninkompoop! You're doing it all wrong!*

Again Fritz shows Wally the proper sequence. When he finishes, he picks up the perfect Widget and shakes it threateningly at Wally. *Last chance, kid!* He walks away.

Fritz changes to WALLY.

Task Mastered

Wally timidly waves goodby to Fritz. When Fritz is safely out of sight, Wally sticks out his tongue. Now he can get back to work.

Wally does it right this time, only very slowly. The second time he does it faster. By the fifth time he's doing it in a blur! He yawns and rolls his eyes. *Big deal. Nothin' to it is right!*

Wally becomes disinterested and lackadaisical. He slows down.

Wally changes to FRITZ.

Worker Motivation

Fritz stands up behind Wally and watches in horror. He chomps, chews, and swallows his cigar, then grabs Wally by the shoulder. *Why so slow? Faster! Faster!*

Fritz dumps huge quantities of materials into Chute A. Again he shakes his finger at Wally and motions for him to move faster. He points a warning at his watch and walks away, muttering and throwing his hands in the air. *People just don't work as hard as they used to!*

Fritz changes to WALLY.

Cooling the Sweatshop

Wally nods his head and, with more than a touch of sarcasm, salutes. But soon the materials come pouring out of the chute, and Wally must work faster and faster. He moves at breakneck speed. Sweat is flying, breathing is short, *I can't take it anymore!*

Soon, the materials come faster than Wally can handle them. He glances once over his shoulder to make sure no one is watching and . . . dumps a load of materials on the floor! He gets quite a giggle out of his actions! This enables him to move at a more leisurely speed. Complete a widget, dump a load of material, complete another widget, dump a load.

Wally changes to FRITZ.

Fritz sneaks up behind Wally and sees what's happening. He's only been playing with anger up to this point. He is now quite serious about it. He grabs Wally by the neck and shakes him violently while pointing at the dumped materials. *You dumb cog!*

Fritz changes to WALLY.

Wally jerks about as though he doesn't have a backbone. Despite the rough treatment (or maybe because of it), Wally gets another bright idea. He points up at the chute. *There's the problem. Not me. The Chute. Go look for yourself!*

Wally changes to FRITZ.

The Widget According to Wally

Fritz quits shaking Wally and looks up at Chute A. He doesn't see that anything's wrong. Reluctantly, he climbs up a little ladder and peers down inside. Nothing. From below, Wally urges him to look deeper. *All right, kid, I'll look, but if there ain't nothin' wrong, you're back in the unemployment line!*

Fritz changes to WALLY.

Wally grins and rubs his hands. He quickly reaches up and pushes Fritz into the chute! When he sees Fritz drop out of the chute, he goes into the assembly line procedure! Just like a pro! To top it off, Wally gets such a chuckle out of kicking Lever H, he gives it a couple of extra boots!

So long Foreman Fritz! I think you'll need a replacement soon, and I think I will be the new foreman!

The Juggler

Opening Jitters

Juggle bug Carla pops out on stage with a big flashy entertainer's smile. She takes a deep bow and encourages the audience to applaud for her. *Come on, louder! Can you not see that I am the great and famous Carla! That's better!*

After thanking the audience for her applause, Carlo grabs the handles of a large cart and rolls it out to center stage. She reaches in and pulls out a small ball (about the size of a tennis ball). She points to the ball and to herself, always with the flamboyant gestures of a bigtime showperson. *And now, I, Carla, will juggle for you!* Pause. *Ah, but first you must applaud! Thank you.*

Carla begins juggling the one ball! Well, at least she *tries* to juggle. She looks like a grounded fish throwing the ball up and struggling to catch it. Her brave smile turns nervous and apologetic. A wild throw . . . she races to catch it . . . trips!

Two Are Better Than One

Carla walks back to the cart and catches her breath. *Just hold on folks! I was only teasing! (I hope!) I will now juggle TWO balls!*

In a flash she pops two balls in the air, catching one, throwing the other, catching one, throwing the other, on and on! She struggles a bit at first, but quickly catches the rhythm. *I must be going deaf? Where's my applause?*

After her first round of claps, she tries a few fancy tricks; under the leg, behind the back, eyes closed, arms crossed.

After this virtuoso display, she stops juggling and looks at the audience. *I've got a surprise for you! How about it? Want to see me juggle . . . are you ready? . . . THREE BALLS!? You do? Then here we go!*

Again, she has some initial difficulties, but soon masters the task and does some showing off. She finishes, takes a quick bow, and indicates she'll do one more trick. *FOUR BALLS! Watch carefully now!*

Juggling four balls is real work for Carla. Her face shows the concentration. She finishes, takes a bow, and starts to push the cart offstage when someone in the audience yells for her to do five balls. In this instance, her mime partner Wally was seated amidst the throng and did the yelling. When she works alone, she just "pretends" to hear someone yell.

Always Leave 'Em Wanting More

Carla stops and looks at the audience with a bit of confusion. *Er, what's that? You want me to juggle five balls? Gee, I thought I gave you a good show, but okay, why not. Just this one time, though!*

She carefully counts out five balls and begins juggling them. She finishes, catches them in her arms, and turns to her cart. *Whew! This juggling is hard work!*

Wally shouts out from the crowd and Carla's head snaps around. *What! You want me to juggle SIX BALLS?* Angrily, she grabs another ball and juggles six. No fooling around here, this is some *serious* juggling! She finishes, doesn't wait for applause, and turns for the cart.

Wally shouts and Carla freezes. She turns around very slowly and faces the audience. She's a little bit afraid of that mob out there. *A minute ago they were in the palms of my hands. Now maybe I'm in their greedy little palms.*

Again Wally shouts. Carla sneers and counts out on her fingers: *TEN BALLS! I don't want to, but . . .*

She plucks out four more balls and begins juggling. Her arms move like high speed motors, throwing, catching, throwing, catching, throwing . . . Lookout! Carla, struggling to maintain control, veers to her left, then right, then . . . CRASH! The balls fall to the floor, giving Carla a headache while trying to keep track of their bouncing.

Or Leave 'Em Wanting Less

The Great Juggling Carla is washed up, defeated. She wowed 'em with three, but fizzed with ten. With shoulders drooping and head hanging low, she shuffles slowly back to her cart. She takes hold of the handles and begins pushing . . . but wait! An idea! A sneaky idea.

You want me to juggle, right? One ball? No, not enough. Two? Not enough. Three? Ha! Ten? No way. How about . . . Carla looks from side to side and flashes ten fingers. And ten more! And ten more! She is going to juggle thirty balls! *How about that? Is that enough? It is? Good!*

She fills her arms with balls, continually glancing with evil sneers at the audience. *Here we go!* She throws the balls up one at a time . . . and when they come down, she catches them and throws them at the audience! *Here's one for you, Wally! And you people in the front row! And you in the back! Take this, take that! Are you satisfied now? Is that enough? Good!*

With a satisfied smile, Carla strolls offstage.

DOING DOUBLE (AND THEN SOME)

Two Mimes

Wally Says:

This is a fun routine to use for an opener, or better still, for the last routine of the first half of your show or the first routine of the second half! Practice your timing, and speak clearly. Not only are you not used to talking, but your audience isn't used to listening!

Suspension of Disbelief

Boxed-in Beliefs

Poor Molly. She's stuck inside a box and can't get out! She traced her boundaries with her hands, defining walls, ceilings, and corners. She tries pushing against the walls, but nothing happens. Undaunted, she continues pushing.

Meanwhile, who should come strolling on stage but good old Wally. He walks right by Molly without noticing her, then stops dead in his tracks. He turns slowly and looks at her. And then . . . surprise of surprises . . . he speaks! That's right! Opens his mouth and makes sounds!

"What on earth are you doing scrunched up like that on the stage floor? Have you got stomach cramps?" Wally is both genuinely shocked and puzzled.

Molly rescrunches to face Wally. She pounds on the box and pleads with him. *Help me! I'm stuck inside this box!*

This Dummy Isn't Stupid!

Wally can't believe what he's seeing! He doesn't know whether to laugh or to be offended.

"What do you take me for, a dummy? You want me to think you're stuck inside one of those invisible mime boxes, don't you? Ha! I've got more brains that that!"

Molly looks at the audience and gestures with her hand. *Close call. Maybe he does have brains, maybe he doesn't.*

Wally starts chuckling and turns away. Frantically, Molly pounds on the box. *Help me!* Wally impatiently turns around.

"Quit bothering me, would you?" He looks down at Molly, who holds her hands up to him in prayer.

"Oh, geez! I'm only going along with this so you'll leave me alone." Wally bends over and "grabs" the box. Molly shakes her head and indicates his arms are too wide apart. "Oh, excuse me," laughs Wally, "I guess I didn't 'see' the right size! Ha!" He lifts the box up and throws it away. Molly watches it crash, shudders, and stands up, finally free. She takes Wally's hand, shakes it, and thanks him profusely.

Mime Mocking

"Spare me the theatrics, please," says Wally. "This mime stuff is a bunch of baloney and I don't like its taste. There wasn't a box on top of you!"

Molly can't believe it! *Really? No box?*

"Not at all. You merely *thought* there was a box on top of you. You were trapped by your own imagination!"

Molly cringes and shies away from Wally. She's not only afraid of what he's saying, but a little angry at him for pointing it out. *And I thought everything was just fine!*

"That's what I don't like about you crazy mimes. You're always pretending things are happening to you! Pretending you're somebody you're not! Delusions of grandeur! Wallowing in self-pity! That's sure not my cup of tea!"

When in Rome . . .

Cup of tea? Coming right up!
Molly takes a kettle of hot water from the stove and pours a

cup of tea for Wally. He rolls his eyes when she hands it to him. He takes it and smirks.

"This is exactly what I'm talking about! This mime business is for little kids. Fairy tales. Am I really supposed to believe that this is a cup of tea?"

Molly nods yes. *Drink it, it's good. Yum!*

Wally laughs again. "I'm telling you I don't believe in this stuff, and I'll bet you don't, either. You're just playing out a fantasy."

Oh, no, no, this is good tea!

"Come on, I'll show you how much you really believe in this malarkey!"

A Splash of Indifference

Wally throws the cup of hot tea in Molly's face!

Molly grabs her face and curls up in pain. She falls to the floor and thrashes and flails.

Wally, meanwhile, chortles nonchalantly.

"You think I was born yesterday or something? You're not in any pain because I didn't throw anything on you! But go ahead and play your little games if you want."

Wally faces the audience and shakes his head. "I'm not a guy who likes to play games. I'm a realist, know what I mean? A dollar in the hand is worth a dream in the sky. Just give me the facts, the nitty gritty, that's all I care about. I don't have time to indulge in these fantasies. They're a waste of time. My time, your time, everyone's time. If people just stuck to the here and now, this old world would be a lot better off."

Paid Back with Interest

While Wally pontificates, Molly recovers and crawls a good ways behind him. She wipes off the hot tea and listens to what he's saying. *Is he crazy? No time to indulge in fantasies? What kind of life is that? I'm beginning to hate this guy. He's dangerous! He needs to be taught a lesson.*

Molly grabs a sheathed sword, straps it to her waist and moves to Wally's side.

"Face isn't so bad after all, is it? Heh, heh!"

Molly draws the sword and aims it at Wally.

"Oh, revenge, is it? Go ahead and prick my imagination. Won't hurt me!"

Molly walks behind him while he smugly chuckles. To test him, she pokes him in the bottom with the tip of the sword. Wally yelps, jumps, and grabs his wounded flank. "Pinching me, are you?" He turns and sees she is standing a sword's length away. She pokes him again. This time he yelps with real fear.

"Hey, what's going on here? I told you I don't believe in this mime stuff! It's not real! It's useless! What you don't know can't hurt you!"

Oh yeah? Molly smiles grimly and makes a final lunge through Wally's heart. Wally staggers and falls to the floor.

"What you don't know can't hurt you! Isn't that right?"

He falls dead. Molly bends over him and shakes her head. *Nope. Sorry. You were wrong.*

She turns and looks at the audience. *And how about you? Do you believe?*

Carla Says:

This is a classic routine popular with all audiences, especially children. We hope you like our own special little twist! By the way, this routine merits plenty of practice if you want to master that "strung out" style . . .

Puppet Pair Parted!

Hanging Out

The two marionettes, Carla and Larry, are fast asleep in a sitting position. Carla's head rests on Larry's shoulder. One of Carla's elbows is held high by a string, and one of Larry's hands is pointing heavenward, also held taut by a string.

All in all, Carla and Larry look like a cozily nestled pair of marionettes. Until . . .

Wake Up Time

The string holding Larry's upraised hand breaks! BONK! It falls and hits Larry on the noggin, then tumbles limply into his lap. *Ooch! Mmm . . . what the . . . ?*

Larry shakes the head and slowly wakes up. He's in a daze at first, trying to figure out where he is, and what he is! At first, he moves only the arm that is still attached to a string. He feels the floor, his face, the string that holds his head, his other arm . . . *Hey! What's wrong with my arm! It doesn't move! It might as well be a wet washrag! Now why . . . oh! There's no string!*

Larry looks all about for the string but can't find it. Finally he looks up. *There it is!* He reaches for it and is just able to grab it. *Now to tie it back!* But the string won't reach down to his fallen arm! He tries lifting his arm with his mouth, but is unable to tie a knot with only one hand. *If only I had a third hand!*

A Helping Hand

Larry looks over at Carla and sees her hand dangling down from her lifted elbow. Thinking one hand is as good as another, he grabs it and puts it on his limp arm to help tie the knot. When he lets go, her hand slides off. He tries again and again, succeeding only in frustrating himself.

Larry eventually turns to Carla and examines her more closely. He decides to shake her around a little bit and wake her up, but finds she's out like a brick. Undaunted, he tugs on the string attached to her head. Lifts it, lets it drop, lifts it, lets it drop, lifts it . . . *She's awake!*

The Little Fix

Even though Carla is a little groggy at first, Larry wastes no time in getting her to help. *Put your finger here, hold tight, and presto! I'm all fixed!* The arm is now working!

Happy as heck, Larry tries to stand on his feet. He helps himself by tugging on his leg strings, and the string attached to his back side. *Whoops!* He pulled a little too hard on the back string and now finds himself standing on his tiptoes! He almost lifted himself off the ground. He finds himself slowly spinning on his toes and stretching his legs for a better contact with the floor. That failing, he desperately yanks *down* on the back string. Plonk! The string lowers, but so does Larry. With a few more tugs, he eventually gets himself set at the right level.

Join the Crowd

Hey you! Down below! Stand up and join me?
Larry gives Carla a few nudges and urges her to stand up.

It's fun! I mean, I am a little wobbly, but I don't have to worry about falling over! To illustrate his point, he leans first to one side and then to the next. When he reaches the maximum leaning point, he simply grabs a string and pulls himself upright. *Simple! No problem!*

Carla giggles and shrugs. She's still a little frightened at the prospect, but gives it a go anyway. Larry helps her to her feet. *This is easier than I thought!* She too is a bit wobbly.

They each spend a moment taking hesitant steps, lifting and dropping their arms, bending over, swinging their legs, all the while observing how they are limited by the strings that hang down *from above.* It's grand fun for both!

Gone Waltzabout

Feeling frisky, Larry lifts Carla's back string so that she has to struggle to keep her toes touching the ground. *Put me down, you silly guy, you!*

Larry agrees, but only if Carla consents to dance with him. He spins around her in a simple waltz step.

Again, Carla is reluctant to try anything new. She shakes her head and declines. But Larry is not one to be denied. He takes her in his arms! They're dancing.

Carla giggles again. *This isn't so bad after all!*

Around and around they go, bouncing and jangling and spinning on the ends of the strings *from above.*

Knot Now!

Whoops again! After a flurry of turns and spins, their strings get tangled with each other's. They're stuck!

Oh, I knew I shouldn't have danced! Carla isn't giggling now.

Larry gets an idea. While standing intertwined and knotted with Carla, swaying at the end of the strings, he begins to untie a string from his head.

Carla is aghast. *What are you doing! Stop! Stop!*

Boink! The string is loose! But so is his head, which rolls to one side. He pushes it with his hand, but still it remains limp. Finally, with great effort, he lifts his head with his own neck! *Wow! This is great! It's easy!*

Prometheus Unstrung

In no time at all Larry unties the rest of his strings. It takes him a moment to learn to control his own body, but when he does, he feels like a superpuppet. *Like a real person!* He leaps and runs and jumps and spins and tumbles and twists! He could never do these things while connected to all of those strings!

Crash! He runs smack into Carla, who is still tangled and stuck in spot. *Sorry. Here, let me untie you!*

But Carla, who isn't giggling now, is frightened to death at the prospect of being untied. *Leave me alone!* She squirms and twists.

Larry shrugs his shoulders and gestures. *What have you got to lose? How about just one string?* Without waiting for her consent, he unties an arm string. And it works for her, too! In seconds she gains control of her own arm. She can't help giggling. She waves it around and makes big flourishes, ending by holding out her hand for Larry to kiss.

Really? Why but of course, madame. He bows and gently kisses. He then quickly unties the rest of Carla's strings! She quickly discovers the freedom of an unstrung body. Together they romp across the floor, laughing and leaping.

They freeze! *What's that? A noise! From over there!*

Larry takes Carla by the hand and runs away . . . *tries* to run away. Carla stops, stares quietly into his face, and quietly looks into his face. *I can't run away. This is where I belong. I'm a marionette. This is where I belong.* She reaches up for her strings, untangles them, and begins reattaching them to her body.

Larry is frantic. The noise is coming closer and they both turn their heads to look. Only a moment left. Carla moves faster. *Come on, let's go! Don't tie yourself up! Down! We're free! Let's go!*

She pauses before tying the last string to her hand. She holds the free hand out to Larry for one last kiss. Resigned to the fact that she won't leave with him, he sadly kisses her one last time. He then gently ties the string to her hand.

Oh! What am I going to do! He walks over to his strings and considers tying himself back up, but declines. *I'd like to stay with her, but I just can't!* He turns back to Carla to explain, but finds her limp and fast asleep.

The noise again! He hasn't any more dilly dally time, so he runs away.

Good-by! Good-by!

An Extra Ending:

New Friends for Old

After Larry, ex-marionette, runs away, Wally, the store owner, enters and sets an OPEN sign on a chair. He's ready to do business. *I'm ready to sell toys! Trains, balls, soldiers, puppets . . . PUPPETS! One's missing!*

As Wally runs over to investigate, who should walk into the store but Larry! He's just another casual consumer looking for a different way to spend money. He walks around, checking toys, whistling. When he sees Carla, the marionette, he stops and looks perplexed. *Haven't I . . . Haven't I met you somewhere before?*

Wally notices Larry's interest and immediately forgets his own problems. *You like? You buy? Yes? No? Good quality. Watch. Er, say, do I know you from somewhere? No? Hmm.*

Wally lifts the control strings off a rack above the marionette's head and operates them. Carla stands, bows, walks, and moves her arms. Wally is pleased with himself. *See? Isn't that what you've always wanted?*

But Larry isn't sure. He turns his back on Wally and the marionette, and Wally, frustrated, looks down at his feet. Meanwhile, the marionette, all on her own, lifts her arm and taps Larry on the shoulder. Larry turns around and finds a hand waiting to be kissed. He chuckles. *Very clever, Mr. Businessman! Okay, what the heck, I'll buy the marionette. Here's your money.* Larry hands the money over, takes the control strings, and walks the marionette out of the store.

Mirror, rorriM

Comb Your Teeth, Brush Your Hair

Groggy-eyed, Larry crawls out of bed and shuffles over to the bathroom mirror. On the other side is his mirror image (as portrayed by Wally). *Ugh! Do I really look that bad?* Larry shakes his head with a shiver of revulsion.

Better to keep busy. He turns on the faucet, fills his hands with cold water, douses his face. *Brrr! They sure don't make water as warm as they used to!*

(Meanwhile, Wally continues to match Larry's movements with uncanny accuracy.)

Larry rolls his tongue over his teeth. *Yick!* He picks up a toothbrush and brushes his teeth. Before spitting, he tilts his head back and gargles. He then bends over the sink, spits, and washes his mouth clean. Wally, however, *doesn't* bend over. He simply swallows and smiles. When Larry stands straight, he peers at his mirror image. *Something's funny here. No, couldn't be! I'm, y-a-w-n, still a little groggy, that's all.*

Larry picks up a comb and straightens his hair out: neat and flat. Meanwhile, Mr. Mirror Image ruffles his hair: wild and electric. *Now doggone it!*, thinks Larry, *I thought I had that cowlick licked!* He tries again, and this time the mirror image complies.

Larry frowns. *I don't feel right about this.* He turns around (almost catching Wally off-guard!) and examines his image. He's confused and confounded. He scratches his chin and peers intently at himself in the mirror. He pulls his hand away . . . and Wally continues to scratch for a brief moment longer!

Larry jumps! (as does Wally). *Am I seeing things, or just living in the past? Hmm. I wonder.*

Larry slowly turns his back to the mirror, as does Wally. Wally giggles, then sighs with relief. *Whew! That was a close call!* Out of the corner of his eye he sees . . . !

Larry turns back around, looks into the mirror, and sees Wally's back. When Wally sees this, he quickly turns around. Too late! Larry is on to the game!

Coming Out

Larry leans forward to study his image more closely. He rubs his hand over his chin and face. Suddenly, he claps his hands and spins around! *Did my image follow me? Yes? Well, let's see if it can follow this!* Thus begins Larry's challenge to the image. He goes through a series of movements and gestures trying to trip up the image. He snaps his fingers, dances, laughs, cries, jumps, spins, waves his arms, makes funny faces, and even tries holding perfectly, absolutely still. Nothing doing.

Larry decides on another tactic: pain. He lightly slaps his own face. His mirror image does the same. Larry slaps again, only a little harder, and again the image duplicates. Larry winces. *This is beginning to hurt!* Larry winds up for a powerful blow. So does the mirror image. The only difference is that the image doesn't want to hit himself. The image hits Larry on the left side of his face as Larry hits his own right side.

Although half-conscious, Larry was prepared for such a turn of events. He grabs Wally's arm and yanks him out of the mirror!

Hi, my name's Id. And you're . . . Ego, I presume?

Even though Wally is out of the mirror, he continues to duplicate Larry's actions. The two are wary of each other and circle slowly. Larry is not at all sure what to do. *Best to keep busy . . .*

He backs up, bends over, and picks up a shoe, puts it on his left foot. Wally does the same, except that the shoe goes on his right foot. Larry is outraged! *Hey! That's my shoe! Give it back!* Larry charges towards Wally, grabs his right leg, and yanks off the shoe. Of course, Wally does the same to Larry.

Larry puts his hands on his hips and displays his anger. *Now see here, whoever you are, this is my home, and that is my shoe.* Wally simultaneously makes the same proprietary claim. *No, no,* explains Larry, *you don't understand. This is MY home, MY shoe, MY . . .*

Wally matches Larry's intensity, but when Larry puts his head in his hands, Wally finds time for a quick giggle. *Boy, am I putting the wool over this guy!*

Larry turns back to Wally.

Duel of the Duplicitous Duo

No longer are their movements synchronized. Each now has control over himself (much to Wally's thanks).

Larry points to the mirror. *You! Back where you belong! This is my home, and that is your home. Now!*

Wally can't help chuckling. Me? Now why would I want to go back there? He shivers and shakes his head in revulsion. No, friend, it's your turn. He pats Larry on the shoulder and points at the mirror.

Larry is understandably upset, but it doesn't stop Wally from giving him a forceful shove into the mirror. It's a short struggle, delayed long enough only for Wally to remove the other shoe.

How do you like them apples, eh? asks Wally of Larry. Wally

chuckles. Larry must now struggle to duplicate Wally's actions, which he does with a sad frown.

Gotta go! Be seeing you! With a snappy wave, Wally turns and walks away. Larry looks after him, his hands and face pressed against the glass.

Another Ending

Wally and Larry are struggling, fighting for possession of the other shoe. They tumble, twist, and roll, and suddenly, in a blink of an eye, the fight is over. They've *merged!* (Wally's front is pressed tight against Larry's back, from the tips of his toes to the tips of his fingers!)

Larry stands up and looks for Wally. *I must have been daydreaming. Whew!* He puts both hands on his hips (while Wally scratches Larry's head!). *Yeah, must have been daydreaming.* And with that, he/they is/are off!

The Big Scare

The Little Sneak

Shhh! Carla holds her finger to her mouth and urges the audience to be quiet. *Good.* Now she creeps silently on her toes to a far corner and hides behind a big box. *Oh, this'll be great! Ha ha!*

No sooner does she hide than does Molly come traipsing in, blithely unaware of the little sneak behind the box. *I'm beat!* She takes off her sweater, stretches. *I'm exhausted!* She pulls up a chair and sits down. *I'm pooped!* She takes out a book and starts reading. *I'm fizzed!*

Super Sneak

Carla peers over the edge of her box and sees that Molly is reading. *Darn! I've got to get her over here! I've got it!* Carla cups her hands around her mouth and pretends to make noises: slow, undulating, eerie.

Molly looks over her shoulder. *What the heck is that?* She tries to ignore the noise, but can't. It proves . . . disconcerting.

I'd better find out what this is all about. She puts her book down and walks toward Carla. Molly walks slower and slower, and becomes more frightened with each step. She passes Carla without seeing her (much to Carla's pleasure) and stops. *I don't see anything. . . .*

Carla stops making the noise and stands up behind Molly, crouched, ready to spring. When Molly turns, Carla jumps in the air and screams! Molly jumps just about as high in fright, and then crumbles to a tiny, shaking bundle.

I got you good!, shouts Carla, dancing around Molly and laughing! *I got you . . . oh dear . . .* Carla sees that Molly was frightened out of her wits (not that she ever had many) and apologizes. *Hey, just a joke. I'm sorry, honest.*

Sore Loser

Molly gets to her feet and snarls. She doesn't find getting scared particularly funny, thank you! It makes her mad! Carla tries to apologize, but to no avail. Molly will have nothing to do with her. She turns her back on Carla and walks out the door.

Carla is crestfallen. *Gee. I was only having some fun. I didn't want to make her mad. I mean, I didn't do anything that* bad. *Oh well. It'll be all right.*

Carla shrugs and sits herself on Molly's chair. She finds the discarded book there, picks it up, and starts reading. It must be one of those hot romance novels, because she's riveted to the pages in a few seconds. Her lips can barely keep up with the action!

A Boo for a Boo, an Eek for an Eek

While Carla is lost in the tongue challenging rapture of the book, Molly (!) creeps back into the room. *Shh!* She cautions the audience to keep her presence a secret. Setting her eyes on Carla, she grins and wrings her hands. *My turn!*

Molly gets to her hands and knees and crawls behind Carla. As Carla reaches a climactic passage, Molly puts her arm over the chair and grabs Carla's shoulder. Carla freezes. She looks at the hand on her shoulder and back at the book, trying to differentiate reality from fantasy. Differentiation complete, she leaps in the air, throws the book, and screams. Molly pops up from behind the chair and laughs. *It's not so fun getting scared, is it?*

Carla is visibly upset, but is able to realize that Molly has simply settled the score. She can't be too mad. They shake hands, give each other a hug, and decide to be better friends in the future.

Gotta Go!

After all is settled, Molly looks at her watch. Gads! She simply *has* to go. *Ta ta 'n' toodles!*

Carla sits down and resumes reading the book. Molly opens the door and ... *AAAAAAAAAAAAAAA!!!* Her mouth falls open and she crumbles to her knees, trembling and shaking, unable to take her eyes off the giant *thing* before her. She points at it and screams again, trying to catch Carla's attention.

Carla wasn't born yesterday. She knows Molly is trying to pull her leg. Frankly, she's a little annoyed. *Come on, enough is enough. I'm trying to read this book.*

Something grabs Molly by the neck and begins choking and shaking her. Her struggles are in vain, and she fights less and less as she is dragged away, off the stage. Carla, still lost in her book, waves for Molly to shut the door. Nothing. Carla looks up and rolls her eyes in disgust. All right, I'll do it myself. She puts the book down and stomps over to the door, grabs the handle, and swings it shut. Halfway back to her chair she stops and her eyes go wide. *Wait a minute! I saw something! Or did I?*

She shakes her head, laughs nervously, and walks back to the door, which she opens. She *did* see something! Something frightening, something big, something monstrous, something that makes her legs shake and her hands clutch her head, something that makes her stumble slowly back into the room.

As the lights fade to black, Carla emits a real, bloodcurdling scream . . .

Larry Says:

This routine is for three or more people. You'll need a few props: a large jar, vase, or box with small sticks in it (one stick being visibly shorter than the others), and plain, clear plastic face masks for each mime. These masks are available in most theater, novelty, or magic stores and are effective in giving an element of eeriness to the characters. If you can't find masks, you can make a head and face covering from an old pair of nylons. Just cut the foot off and slip it on. You might also wish to experiment with special lighting and long robes.

The Sacrifice

The Gathering

The Leader stands alone in the center of the stage. His back is bent and his head hangs low. He is a tired, weary person. He sighs deeply, looks to his side, and beckons the others to come join him.

They shamble forth, tired followers all. Their heads, masked (like the Leader's) and bent, bob back and forth. They are virtually indistinguishable from one another and huddle together, clinging and tugging at one another comfort and security. Their movement is slow and plodding.

The Prayer

When they join the Leader, he turns his back to them and looks up at the idol. He lifts his arms in praise and timidly steps forward. At the base of the idol he begins bowing from the waist. Slowly at first, then more and more rapidly. One by one, the followers join in the practice.

The Leader falls to his knees and continues the rapid bowing. The other follow. The Leader prostrates himself, stretches his arms forward, and rapidly slams the floor with his arms and legs. The others follow. The pounding reaches a feverish pitch, continues a brief moment, then suddenly ends. Prayer is finished, and the Leader and the followers catch their breaths and regain their strength.

The Ax

Eventually, after a brief period of groping about on the floor, the Leader stands and treads off to a far corner. The followers get to their knees and form a tight group. They watch the Leader lift an ax, test the sharpness of the blade with his thumb, and swing it down, hard, into a stump.

The Lottery

The Leader now moves to the front of the stage. He picks up the box that contains the sticks and holds it high, facing the followers. They begin to shake, and shake their heads in nervous little jitters.

But when the Leader holds forth an angry fist, they crawl forward. They move as a group, sometimes crawling over their own, sometimes dragging the unwilling. When they reach the feet of the Leader, they cover their heads and shake with fear.

The Leader grabs a follower by the scruff of the neck, lifts him to his feet, and holds the box before him. Nervously, the follower starts to reach in, pulls back, then quickly makes a grab. He's pulled out a long straw. The follower is relieved. He holds the straw high, in awe, and slowly wanders off to a distant point in the room, never taking his eyes off his straw.

The other followers do the same, each pulling a long straw, each feeling relief. Finally there is but one follower. He is very frightened and refuses to reach into the box, despite being kicked and beaten by the Leader. The Leader calls to the others and they join him, circling around the unwilling follower and urging him to draw. They, too, beat and kick him.

The Last Straw

The victim can bear it no longer. Not only can he not bear the physical pain, but he can't bear the spiritual repression. He jumps to his feet, proud, tall, erect. The others, even the Leader, cower before him. They point at him and nervously shake their heads. And then . . . *then* . . . they watch motionless as he lifts his hands to his mask and very, very slowly removes it.

Freedom

He is now the Unmasked. The others cover their faces and refuse to look at him. He too is somewhat fearful. This is a new experience. He checks over his shoulder to see if there are any approaching lightning bolts (or comparable threats). When he realizes nothing will happen, he gently touches his face, explores it, and decides he likes it. *Likes.*

For the first time, he smiles. It's a shy smile at first, but it quickly widens into a big grin. He laughs! He bellows! He guffaws! He is happy!

The others, including the Leader, now dare to look at him, and only occasionally cover their masked faces.

But the Unmasked! He leaps with joy! He twirls, bounces, dances, makes silly faces, mocks the Leader and the followers, sticks his rear end up at the idol, and thoroughly enjoys his new view on life. He waltzes over to his old mask, picks it up, giggles, and gives it a healthy kick. Words do not exist to describe the shock and disgust of the Leader and the followers.

The Leading Edge

While the Unmasked frolics and teases the followers, the Leader slowly makes his way to the ax. He picks it up, retests the sharpness. That finished, he carries the ax back to the followers. They huddle together and listen to the Leader. They obey: They slowly circle the Unmasked so that he can't escape. He lets them grab him and drag him to the box. Here he struggles as they grab his arm and shove it into the box. He shuts his eyes, grits his teeth, and grabs a straw. It is a short one. He loses.

The Unmasked laughs again and turns to the Leader. He doesn't care about their silly little rituals, he's free. He's happy and that's what is important. They can take his life, but they can't take away his happiness. He fills his chest and holds his chin high in proud defiance.

The Cutting Edge

His defiance is met. The followers grab him and hold him face down on the floor. The Leader offers a final prayer to the idol and then swings the ax.

The Leader removes the ax. When he does, he carries it back to where he found it, then returns to the followers and the body. With a sigh, he picks up the discarded mask, puts it back on the face of the dead man, and gestures for the others to follow him. They pick up the dead man and carry him away, to wherever sacrifices are deposited.

Wally Says:

This is fun! All I have to do is act like I do at home!

Larry Says:

Er, there's a little more to it than that. First, the Grim Reaper (my part) should wear a long, hooded robe. A scythe is a nice extra touch, but not absolutely necessary. A few extra title cards will help explain locales. An assistant is helpful for carrying the cards but, if you don't have one, not required.

The Grim Reaper and the Empty Harvest

This Is the Life!

"A can of beer, a jar of peanuts, and thou, televizing before me." This is pretty much Wally's motto, and he lives by it as best he can.

He walks into his room, pops the lid off a can of beer, takes a swig, and turns on the television. He pats his big, round belly while the set is warming up and emits a cheek puffing belch. *Ah, life is good! If only I didn't have this darn pain in my chest. No big deal . . .*

He spins the dial, finds a good station, and settles back in his easy chair to enjoy the good life. He finishes his can of beer and starts in on another . . . never taking his eyes off the tube. He grabs a jar of nuts and munches on them for a while. He lights a cigarette. Between the actions of chewing, smoking, and drinking, Wally's face falls into the dangle-jawed tv trance.

Time Traveler

While Wally is entranced in the world of the glowing tube, an assistant walks across the stage holding a large title card: LATER THAT WEEK . . .

Wally continues his endeavors, pausing only to crush an empty beer can and toss it aside.

A moment later, the assistant walks across the stage holding a card: LATER THAT MONTH . . .

Wally lifts one of his haunches, scrunches his face, then sighs with relief and reseats himself. He absently massages his chest.

The assistant walks by with another card: LATER THAT YEAR . . .

Wally guzzles off the last of the beer and opens another. He gets up to change the channel on the television. Before sitting down again, he stretches his left arm and tries to work out a cramp. He sits down, rubs his chest again, and gets back to the jar of nuts.

The assistant walks through with yet another card: LATER THAT DECADE . . .

Wally reaches to open another can of beer when a particularly bad pain makes itself known in his chest. He grabs at his heart and grimaces. *Heart attack! Just the way it happens to those guys on tv!*

A Visitor Arrives

Wally looks up and sees . . . DEATH! The Grim Reaper stands in front of the television, his face hidden in the darkness of the hooded robe. He moves slowly, *just like I always thought he would!*

He points off to the distance and with one finger beckons Wally to join him. But Wally shakes his head. *No, no, please don't make me go now! I'm too young!*

The pain disappears and Wally stands up. He takes a quick drink of beer and makes his case. There are so many things he hasn't had a chance to do! *Things like . . . well . . . I know!* He acts his wishes out for the Grim Reaper's benefit: ride a bicycle, fly an airplane, climb a mountain, have a wife and a baby, ride a horse, go fishing, read books and think, go scuba diving. All kinds of things!

Won't you please give me a second chance, Mr. Grim Reaper? Please? Pretty Please? With cherries on top?

A Second Chance

The Grim Reaper sighs deeply and gives pause to think. He slowly nods his head one time and walks away. Wally is overjoyed! *Oh, hey, thanks, I really appreciate this. Say, wanna take a can of beer with you?*

The Grim Reaper continues walking without acknowledging Wally's gesture. Wally shrugs. *Suit yourself! Just one more for me!*

Old Habits

As soon as the Grim Reaper is gone, Wally chuckles, rubs his hands together, and gets back to business: watching television, drinking beer, eating nuts, belching . . .

I sure put one over on that Mr. Grim Reaper! Ha!

A moment later, the assistant walks by with another card: LATER THAT LIFETIME . . .

This time the assistant stops directly in front of Wally's television set, and Wally gets mad. He crumples a beer can and throws it at the assistant. *Go on, get out of my way! I'm busy trying to watch this commercial!*

Slightly miffed, the assistant moves on.

An Old Friend

Ouch! Wally grabs at his chest. *It hurts! Ooch! Ouch!*

Wally slumps unconscious in his chair. The Grim Reaper walks in, sees Wally, the beer cans (he even kicks one!), and the television set. He nods his head: *I might have suspected . . .*

He taps Wally on the shoulder and wakes him up. *Time to go.*

Wally jumps up. *Hey, good to see you, old buddy, wanna beer? No, that's right, you don't drink . . . go? . . . aw, but gee, there are so many things I'd like to do. I'd like to go fishing, ride a bike, golf . . .*

The Grim Reaper shakes his head no. He points to the distance and takes Wally by the hand.

Wally shrugs. He's not too upset. He didn't think the Grim Reaper would go for it a second time. Before he takes off, though, he grabs a few more cans of beer and sticks them in his pockets.

The Empty Harvest

Just as Wally and the Grim Reaper exit on one side of the stage, the assistant enters on the other, holding another card: HELL!

The assistant leaves and Wally and the Grim Reaper walk on. The Grim Reaper points to a chair. Wally is a little befuddled. *This is it?* He sits in the chair, picks up a can of beer, and turns on the television set. Looking back at the Grim Reaper, he offers some nuts and the chance to share watching a program. The Grim Reaper is motionless.

The assistant walks by with a card: ETERNAL DAMNATION!

Wally continues munching and viewing and the Grim Reaper cocks his head and occasionally sighs. The assistant walks by with another card: LATER THAT ETERNITY . . .

As she passes by Wally, he snaps his fingers and requests that she change the station. She frowns, but still obliges. *Yeah, that's a good show. Thanks honey!*

After the assistant leaves, the Grim Reaper shakes his head, drops his scythe, and tosses his hands in the air. He scratches his head and tries to figure out what went wrong.

Wally laughs at a funny "television moment," notices the Grim Reaper, and invites him over. He holds up a beer. *Come on, you've got to start drinking sometime.*

The Grim Reaper shrugs in despair and takes a can of beer, as well as a seat in front of the television.

Short Takes #1

Carla Says:

Always a good idea to have a series of quick, snappy routines to perform in succession. It helps give a little variety to the rhythm and pacing of your performance. Not only will the audience appreciate it, but you and your partners will get a quick fix of quickened energy and enthusiasm as well!

The Hunter

The Hunted

Carla the Lion Cat licks her paws and purrs. Just for fun, she extends her claws so that she can admire them. They're long and sharp, and she's understandably proud of them. She puts them back and sniffs the air. What's that? She gets to her feet and snarls. Her eyes catch something and she pounces! *Gotcha!*

Carla the Lion Cat has caught a rabbit. It struggles and takes a few limp swipes at her nose which she has no trouble dodging. After playing with the rabbit for a moment, she licks her lips and opens her mouth wide . . . but wait!

She sniffs the air and smells danger. She lets the rabbit go and looks into the distance. Whack! The rabbit lands a swipe on her nose. Unamused, she lands an even mightier swipe on the rabbit's hindquarters and sends it flying.

She sniffs again and decides she'd better leave at once.

The Hunter

Wally the Hunter enters the stage immediately after Carla the Lion Cat exits. He's hot on the trail, and he senses it. He pulls out his binoculars and scans the wilds. *There it is!*

He's spotted his prey.

He checks his equipment to make sure he's loaded. He's

empty, so he puts in a cartridge. He holds the scope up to his eye and adjusts the focus. Perfect. He's off!

The Chase

Wally storms off the stage, and Carla the Lion Cat enters, checks hurriedly over her shoulder, and quickly exits on the opposite side. Wally is right on her tracks. He enters and exits behind her. Back and forth they go, from one side to another, but always faster and more excited.

The Shoot!

Carla the Lion Cat enters again . . . but can't get out! She's trapped in a tight canyon! She can't even leap or claw her way out! Frightened and angry, she turns to meet her hunter.

Wally enters, grinning from ear to ear! *Oh boy! This'll be fun!* Bringing his hands up, he squints through the scope . . . and snaps a photograph! Great, great! Snap, snap, snap. He adjusts the focus, moves for a better angle, and tries to get Carla the Lion Cat to pose.

Carla emits a halfhearted snarl. *They sure don't make hunters like they used to.* Bored, she lopes away. Wally follows, still clicking his camera.

Filibuster Blusters

Will it never end? Larry enters the stage fighting a ferocious wind. It's a steady movement of air with only occasional gusts. He leans into it at a forty-five degree angle to keep from falling over backwards. His movements are slow. He strains every muscle to proceed forward. His face is scrunched tight.

He makes his way across the stage, every now and then being knocked back a few steps by an especially strong blast.

Bluster Bubble Burster

While Larry is exerting his utmost to merely not lose ground against the wind, who should come strolling along but Molly. Strolling? Strolling! The wind doesn't seem to notice she exists. Not a single strand of hair is out of place.

Molly walks past Larry without noticing him, then stops. Larry looks back at her and frowns. Molly turns around, looks at Larry, catches his eye, and laughs. She points at him and giggles! *Don't you look silly!*

She walks away, still amused.

The Calm Before the Storming Away

Larry looks back at Molly and then at the audience. Though he is still bent forward, he obviously is no longer fighting against the wind. An embarrassed, frightened look comes across his face, and . . . he falls forward, flat on his face. He gets up, sheepishly cleans his pants and shirt, and quickly leaves the stage with as much dignity as he can muster.

Wally Says:

We break the rules here, and utter a short phrase of real words at the end of the routine. But rules are made to be broken, right? If you can figure an equally effective way of silently getting the point across, please let me know . . .

Chess Champions

Grumbling Gambits

Larry and Wally sit across from each other. A chess board sits between them, with the pieces positioned in various locations (somewhere between midgame and endgame).

Larry is absorbed in the game. He clenches his fists, bites his lip, grimaces with thought. His eyes dart about, looking here, looking there, trying to figure out where his opponent will move and how he will counter. *Speaking of moving . . .*

Larry casts an impatient glance at Wally and points at the board. *Come on, hurry it up!*

Wally yawns. He tries to concentrate on the game, really he does! But his intellect is more inclined toward a game of checkers, or better yet, tiddlywinks. He yawns again and starts to reach for a piece, then decides against it. *I bet I'm missing a good television show.*

When the Going Gets Tough . . .

Larry waits on every move, every flicker of action that Wally gives—which are few and far between. Larry taps his fingers. He takes deep breaths. He clears his throat. He twiddles his thumbs. He counts to one hundred. He shuffles his feet. *I can't take it any*

longer! Move! This is a game of thought, intellect, not endurance!
Wally just sits there, looking at the board as if it were a cloud
floating by on a sunny, summer day.

Larry gnashes his teeth and grinds his fists together. He runs
his hands through his hair. *Come on! Move! Move! Put me in mate if
you want, but just move!*
Wally absently scratches beneath his arm. Finally (after he figures he's squeezed every last ounce of patience out of the audience), he looks up at Larry and speaks.
"Am I black or white?"

Larry Says:

It's fun to have someone behind the stage operating a sound effects tape: a cheering crowd, a booing crowd, the crack of the bat, grunting, groaning, and fighting of athletes, buzzers, bells, distant shouts of umpires and referees and whatever else you come up with. Like I say, sound effects aren't necessary, but they're a nice little extra when you've got the time and equipment to create and use them. I also encourage you to use lots of "sportsfan" props.

Sportsfans!

That's My Seat, Bub!

Wally is a true blue (blue-collar, that is) sportsfan. He's loud, emotional, and he loves his team. He walks into the stadium like a true competitor. Today's game is no frivolous match, and neither is Wally there to merely have fun. He intends to do some serious, intense, rooting and rahing. He grabs his pennant as though it were a police baton and pulls out his ticket. *AREA 73, SECTION A44, GROUP RT, BLOCK 981, SUB-SECTION GF 256, ROW CV, SEAT 583592 EH.*

Wally looks up and scans the seats. *Should be right over there.* He works his way through the crowded row, stepping on people's toes, pushing and shoving, and yelling at people who don't get out of his way. *C'mon, mac, I wanna watch the game!*

Wally stops in front of his seat. He knows it is his seat because he can read the number on the ticket. Unfortunately, someone is in his seat. Wally barks at him, but he doesn't move. Only mildly frustrated (for Wally), Wally grabs the fellow by the collar and shoves his ticket in his eye. *That's my seat, see? Now scram.* Wally lifts him and gives him a quick boot to hurry him along. *This is better,* beams Wally, as he settles himself and begins studying the field of play. *Wow! Look at that hit!* Wally jumps up and cheers.

The Professional Fan

Wally is totally immersed in the game by the time Larry arrives. Larry is a pure thoroughbred fan. He's not here to indulge in crude emotional outpouring with the sweaty mob, no, no, not at all. Larry is here to savor the intellectual satisfaction that comes from watching two groups of highly trained men combine agility, physical strength, and mental cunning in a contest of baseball.

Larry is burdened with his professional equipment: thermos, binoculars, radio, visor, notepad, pencil, lunchbox, seat cushion, stopwatch, umbrella, and a few other miscellaneous bags and packs. He doesn't need to look at his ticket to know where his seat is. He has season tickets for SEAT 583592 EH. Struggling to work his way down the row (pausing to apologize to everyone), he eventually finds himself standing directly in front of Wally.

A Lesson in Property Rights

Wally looks up at Larry and snarls. *What is your problem, eh? Can't you see I'm trying to watch my team?*

Larry apologizes, of course, but does deign to offer an explanation. He pulls his ticket out and shows that Wally is sitting in Larry's seat. Wally snorts out a smile of disbelief. He takes out his own ticket and hands it to Larry. *See for yourself. This is my seat.* Larry looks at it and thinks for a moment. He then points to a seat on the far, far side of the stadium. Wally grabs the ticket back and checks again. *Oh, yeah, I guess you're right . . . well, hey, no big deal, you just take this empty seat next to me. Here.*

Larry laughs with quiet embarrassment. *That won't quite do. You see, I chose this seat because it affords optimum viewing.* He holds his arms out wide. *This other seat isn't as good.* He holds his arms out the same distance, then brings them one inch closer together. *So you see, I must have my seat.*

Wally throws his arms high in the air. *I give up. Take it.* As he struggles past Larry and all of his equipment to get into the other seat, he misses a big play. *What happened? Did I miss something? Great, just great.*

Friends in Fandom

Wally can't hold a grudge for long . . . especially when filled with the smugness of superiority that comes from watching a crazy fan unpack two hundred pounds of useless junk. Wally turns to one side and chuckles.

Larry puts the radio earplug in his ear to catch up on the details of the game. He studies the field with binoculars and makes notes on the statistics. Since there is little excitement on the field, Wally spends a good deal of time studying Larry (and trying not to laugh!).

CRACK! A high fly ball sails into right field and is caught. End of inning, and time for Larry's lunch. He opens his lunch box and takes out a tiny, well-wrapped sandwich, then carefully unscrews his thermos and pours a cup of hot coffee. Wally looks on and licks his lips. How can a fellow help getting hungry looking at that food?

Wally rubs his stomach, stands up, and barks out an order to a hot dog vendor. *Ten hot dogs, two beers!* He pulls a bill out of his wallet, passes it down the row. *Ah, here comes lunch!* Wally leans over Larry, anticipating the taste of the approaching food . . . and drools. *Oh dear!*, tuts Larry, and wipes himself clean.

Wally reaches for the food and trips and crashes down on top of Larry. There goes Larry's lunch, including his hot coffee. Hot coffee? *OUCH! That burns! That's hot! That's . . . ahh . . . that's better.* Wally apologizes in passing, then grabs his food and settles himself in his seat.

Larry watches in horror as Wally downs hot dog after hot dog with single gulps. Wally notices Larry watching him. *Oh, hey, gee, I'm sorry, I shoulda offered you one. Here.* Larry, much to his displeasure, is forced to take a hot dog. He nibbles at it, then tosses it over his shoulder when Wally isn't watching.

Back to the Game

Wally claps Larry on the back. *I kinda like you! You're okay, even with all the rigamarole you brought with you. You're a fan of the game, and that's what counts!*

Larry politely nods his head.

Enough for socializing, the game is now in full swing. A hit! Wally cheers and shakes his fist, Larry nods his head (*well done!*) and writes down another statistic. A stolen base! Another hit! A run! Wally is ecstatic and jumps up and down. He pounds poor Larry on the back. Larry doesn't seem to mind, though. In fact, he's rather amused by Wally's antics. *All part of the aura of sports! Another element to be experienced, savoured!*

Turnaround for the Worse

Wally's happiness is something to be shared, by golly! He claps Larry on the back again and tries to get him excited. *Come on, fellow, you're missing all the fun! Throw that junk away and get into the game!*

Unfortunately for Wally, there's not much game to get into at the moment. A strikeout! A grounder right into the first baseman's glove! A pop fly to center! *Geez! What's going on out there? Where'd those guys learn to hit, the School of Nice Manners? Geez oh man!*

The other team comes up to bat and bingo! A hit! Wally covers his face in his hands. Another hit! And another! Wally stomps his feet, shakes his fists, and snarls! *What's this world coming to?* But wait . . . it's worse than he thought.

Beside him, Larry is reluctantly getting caught up in the game! But he's cheering for the wrong team (from Wally's point of view). True, Larry isn't nearly as exuberant as Wally, but he does manage to clap, smile, and even bite his lip as he watches a grounder dodge mitts.

Wally grabs him by the collar. *What are you doing? That's our team that's losing!* Slightly miffed, Larry takes Wally's hand off his collar. Just when they were getting to be friends, too! Larry takes his coat off, folds it, and sets it on his lap.

Seeing Is Disbelieving!

Wally can't believe it! On the front of Larry's shirt is a large "S", the first letter of the opposing team! *The enemy! I'm sitting right next to the enemy!* Wally defiantly takes off his coat, too. *Look at that!* Wally's shirt is emblazoned with a large "B". *And to think I gave you one of my hot dogs! Why I ought to punch you good!*

Larry looks disdainfully at Wally and his raised fist. *Really, my dear man! I had thought better of you than this!*

Wally sulks and puts his fists in his pockets. He shakes his head and avoids looking at Larry. *Okay, so I got a little carried away. I wasn't really going to hit him. Geez, how can anybody like that "S" team!* He looks again at Larry's letter to make sure he didn't misread it. *"S"! Geez!*

Larry shakes his head in sorrow and casts quick glances back at Wally. *Too bad. Seemed like such a nice fellow. I was getting to like him. Oh, well, what can you expect from a man who follows the "B" team. No finesse, no depth, no style . . . and no chance of a pennant. Still, I did envy his ability to totally immerse himself in the game . . .*

Rainy Day Friends

Both Larry and Wally are now watching the game with a certain distance. They're ill at ease sitting next to each other after their little conflict. Wally, perhaps guilty because of his flareup, can't seem to enjoy the game. Larry, having lost the newfound enthusiasm that Wally showed him, doesn't even bother to keep statistics. Ho hum. They happen to turn and accidentally face each other, then quickly turn their heads. Larry frets. *Tsk, tsk, this won't do.*

Plop! Something lands on Larry's head and he turns to Wally. Plop! Something lands on Wally's head and he turns to Larry. *Did you . . .?*
No, but did you . . .?

Plop! Plop! Ploploploplop! It's raining! Satisfied that neither was the cause of the original plop, they quickly grab their coats and cover up. It looks like one heck of a rainstorm moving in. They both shudder and grimace. *Darn! Rained out!*

Larry stands and prepares to leave. He pops open his umbrella, *ah, much better,* and starts to gather his many bags, boxes, and doodads. Wally looks briefly at the umbrella, then turns and slowly walks away. Meanwhile, Larry is having troubles gathering his belongings while holding the umbrella. He picks up one item and drops another.

Wally stops, turns around, and sees Larry fumbling about. Ah, what the hey? He walks back and offers to help carry a few things. They look at each other and smile.

Hey, you're not such a bad guy after all!

Neither are you! Here, share my umbrella!

Don't mind if I do! Whaddya say we grab a beer, huh?

Carla Says:

This is a quick, simple routine that's popular with children. Concentrate on keeping your movements in parallel with your partner's so that you don't accidentally "see" each other. The routine has a simple, cartoon-like plot, so try to keep it short and snappy. Larry wears white, Carla wears black.

The Document

Larry is a seasoned agent for the Acme Espionage Company. He stands in the front left corner of the stage and casts a few surreptitious glances here and there. *Good! I'm all alone!*

He reaches deep into a jacket pocket and slowly pulls out an envelope. Not just any envelope, mind you, but a very important envelope. It contains The Document! He carefully takes it out, reads it, smiles, and rubs his fingers together. *Ah! Power! Wealth! Victory!*

Larry doesn't wallow in glory. Remember, he's a seasoned agent. He folds The Document and puts it safely away in his wall safe. He can't help feeling more secure.

The Other Document

Meanwhile (and simultaneously), Carla stands in the front right corner of the stage. She looks carefully over her shoulder and decides she's alone. *Great!*

She reaches up her sleeve and pulls out an envelope that contains The Other Document! She quickly reads it and glows with glee. *And now I'll hide it where no one can find it! In my safe!*

The Assignment (. . . should they choose to accept)

Both Larry and Carla (whose actions are now clearly established as identical and parallel) receive phone calls. *Hello?* A nod of the head. A gasp of the mouth. Larry points at Carla with shock of what he's been told. He then points to his safe and The Document. He salutes and hangs up. His mission: *Go to her safe, grab The Other Document, bring it back, put it in my safe!*

Carla receives the same assignment from her superior.

Espionage in Action

Carla (as does her counterpart) goes into action. She crouches down and looks everywhere for suspicious characters. She moves to the center, then toward the back, creeping along an invisible wall. When she turns a corner, she leaps out with a gun in her hand, ready to shoot a waiting assailant. Fortunate for the assailant that he's not there!

Larry traces a similar path of stealth. Amazing that they never bump into or see each other!

Safecrackers!

Larry finally reaches his destination: Carla's safe! He crouches down, dons a stethoscope and stretches into rubber gloves. He puts the probe on the safe and turns the dial. Each time a tumbler drops into place his head reverberates. *Ouch! Ooch! Eek! I didn't know spying was harmful to one's hearing!*

Finished! The last tumbler has fallen into place. Larry grabs the handle, turns it, and pulls! He pulls! He pulls harder! He . . . pulls the handle off!

Darn! If the door won't open, I'll make it open! I'll blast it open with dynamite! He promptly puts a stick beneath the safe, lights the fuse, and turns around. Something's wrong. His stethoscope is still attached to the safe! He reaches for it when . . . KABOOM!

Befuddled Backtrackers

KABOOM! Carla's own stick of dynamite explodes and sends her tumbling. She staggers to her feet in a daze and wanders back to the safe. The door now swings gently open. Still semiconscious, she smiles when she grabs The Document. She shuts the door and begins the journey back to her own safe.

Still in a daze, she walks right into Larry (who was equally shaken up by his own explosion). They crash to the floor and rub their sore noses. Slowly, they regain their senses. Carla frantically looks about for The Document, Larry for The Other Document. They each grab the same paper off the floor.

Hey, that's mine!

Ha! Surely you jest! Carla sees another paper on the floor and picks it up to give it to Larry. He reluctantly takes it and lets her have the object of dispute. They each quickly read their papers and scratch their heads. *Gee, this looks awful familiar. I wonder if . . .*

Carla grabs Larry's paper and he grabs hers. They read. Again they scratch their heads. *I can't tell the difference!* They switch again. They join forces in studying the papers. *Is this familiar to you? Do you see any difference?*

They shrug their shoulders and decide The Document is as good as The Other Document. They nod their good-bys and march off to their respective safes where they lock the stolen documents away.

They smile contentedly. *My country is safe, and the enemy has been foiled! I'll sleep well tonight!*

Molly Says:

A snappy routine with a good punch line. Perfect for a large group of performers (or a few "quick change" artists!). You may want to experiment with a large sack or wraparound costumes for the Amoeba and Roach. A good Amoeba costume consists of several large sheets sewn together with enough room inside for three or four people. It should also include holes just large enough for arms and heads to stick out of. A good Roach costume is a large piece of cloth that can be wrapped around two piggybacked torsos.

Wally Says:

It's not strictly kosher according to the rules of mime, but I like to add sound effects for each of the animals *after* they've left the stage. Try it sometime and see how it works! I also suggest title cards to introduce each of the animals.

Food Chain

Jelly Belly

The Official Title Card Holder struts out to the stage and holds up the first card: MR. AMOEBA.

The Amoeba jumps out and lunges (as only amoeba can do) at

the Official Title Card Holder, who quickly dodges away. Inside the Amoeba, which is a very, very large sack, are Larry, Wally, and Molly. They step over each other and roll on the ground, causing the sack to slide and roll forward. Occasionally, one sticks an arm out from the sack to make a grab for the Official Title Card Holder (hereafter, OTCH).

OTCH, thinking she's offended the Amoeba, changes to the next card: MRS. AMOEBA. It doesn't work. The Amoeba makes another lunge. OTCH tries the next card: MISS AMOEBA. Again the Amoeba is angered and grabs for her. Another card: MS. AMOEBA. No luck this time, either. OTCH is running out of stage room and must try to appease the Amoeba's feelings with one last card: AMOEBA PERSON. Success! The Amoeba quiets down. Sighing with relief, OTCH steps around the Amoeba and walks to the far side of the stage (the left, let's say) where she shows another card: THE ROACH.

The Roach charges out from the left. OTCH shudders and quickly disappears. What is the Roach? It's one mime on his hands and knees with another mime trailing directly behind, chest atop the first one's back. A large piece of cloth is wrapped around their torsos to make them appear as one.

A Quick Chase

The Amoeba sees the Roach and shakes with fright. The Roach sets its sights on the Amoeba and begins waving its arms/legs/antennae. It quickly gives chase, forcing the Amoeba off the right side of the stage. The Roach grins and leaps for the final kill. With both of them off the stage, we hear some of Wally's famous sound effects: KRUNCH, SLURP, SQUEAK, WHIMPER, GURGLE, KRUNCH. Your typical roach, amoeba noises.

Out of the Heavens

The Roach walks back out on stage wiping its lips. *Yum!*

At the same time, OTCH walks on and holds another card: THE PIGEON.

The Roach shakes its head in disbelief. *YIKES! Not the Pigeon! Puh-lease!*

After OTCH leaves, the Pigeon struts out, head bobbing with each step, wings folded, cheeks and chest puffing huge and deflating. It sees the Roach and starts to scramble after it. The Roach moves a little quicker than the Amoeba, however, and the Pigeon must take to the air. It flaps its wings a few times and is flying, smooth and graceful. The Roach scurries off the right side and the Pigeon descends. Both offstage, the sounds of a pigeon feast are heard: *Koo! Koo! Chomp! Chomp! Koo! Koo! Burp!*

Filled to the brim, the Pigeon struts back on stage, preening its ruffled feathers. Indigestion soon sets in, unfortunately, when OTCH walks through with another card: FIDO.

Fido is heard offstage: *WOOF! WOOF!*

Fido's Fixin's

Fido romps forth, galumphing on all fours, tongue hanging, lungs panting, tail wagging. Until . . . until he sees the Pigeon. When he does, Fido crouches into an attack position. The Pigeon stops cooing, bobbing its head, preening and puffing. It's in trouble and it knows it. It turns and starts to take flight towards the right side of the stage.

Fido is faster. Charging across the stage, he leaps in the air the instant the Pigeon takes flight. They both disappear offstage.

Fido shares his triumph with a loud WOOF!

When he trots back on stage, however, he finds he feels more like whimpering. OTCH is standing there holding another card: THE LION. Fido looks up at her as if to say, Why me? She shrugs, smiles sadly, and waves good-by.

Boring Roaring

The Lion slinks onto the stage and eyes Fido. The Lion extends his fangs, snarls, and hunches his shoulder muscles. He crouches and springs towards Fido, ready to chase to the end! But Fido, perhaps too full of Pigeon, doesn't want to play the game. He holds up a paw: *Take it easy, Leo, I'm getting too old for this.*

The Lion snarls and snaps at Fido. Fido sighs and quietly trots offstage. The Lion, smacking his lips, makes a final charge: ROAR! ROAR!

Master of the Game

The Lion slowly steps back onstage and takes a big cat nap. He's full and satisfied, as can be seen in the way he licks his paws and claws clean.

With a giant yawn, he falls asleep.

OTCH walks on stage with another card: WEEKEND HUNTER. She walks over to the Lion and notices him sleeping. She gives him a nudge with her foot, trying to warn him of the danger, but all it gets her is a big scratch! *You're on your own, Leo!*

When OTCH leaves, the human Hunter enters. He carries a big rifle and has a round belly. He looks through his binoculars and spots his prey: the Lion. He smiles. *This'll look great on the dining room floor!*

With the Lion sleeping, the Hunter is in no hurry. He pulls out of a can of beer, pops off the tab, and begins chugging. The Lion jerks upright, perhaps because he heard the can opening. Whatever the reason, he sees the Hunter and prepares to attack! The Hunter finishes his beer, crumples the can, and sees he's in big trouble. He struggles to ready his rifle, fumbles, and decides to run. The Lion gives chase and they both disappear.

BANG!

Happy Hunting Grounds

The Hunter frolics back onstage, jumping and laughing! *I got him! I got him! I got—*

Oops! He slips, trips, and falls on his rifle. He accidentally pulls the trigger and shoots himself! *Aargh!*

The First Link Is the Last

Who should come rolling out but the Amoeba? It stops before the dead Hunter, seems to giggle, and rolls on top. It shivers and shakes (while the Hunter is "consumed" through a large hole in the sack!) and moves on. The Hunter is gone!

OTCH walks through with the last card: END OF CYCLE.

Molly Says:

I wouldn't be caught dead performing this routine without my overalls and work cap!

Carpenter Cut Up

Improvisational Architecture

Molly and Carla stand in center of the building plot and unravel a large blueprint. They hold it up so that the audience can read the backside: HOUSE #86. Unable to make any sense out of it, they turn it upside down. Molly scratches her head and shrugs. *It's Greek to me.*

Carla agrees. With a laugh, she wads up the blueprint and kicks it away. *Who needs a plan, anyway? Whaddya say we get this lumber moved into place?*

Work Smart, Not Hard

They walk over to the waist-high stack of lumber and try to lift it. OOOF! It's very heavy. Molly decides to pick one piece off the top, but Carla shakes her head. She points to her watch. *Time is of the essence! We've got to move it all at once.*

Molly reluctantly puts the single piece back on top and moves to the back of the stack. Carla turns around so that her back faces Molly and the stack, and lifts (with lots of grunts and groans) her end of the stack. *Lift your end and let's go!*

Molly deigns to extend her pinky finger to lift one end of the

· 138 ·

top board. *All set at this end!* Carla starts moving, straining and struggling to drag the stack by herself. She stops to catch her breath and turns to check on Molly. Molly quickly pretends to have been struggling along. She pants and wipes her brow.

After more hard labor (on Carla's part), they get the stack moved to the center of the plot.

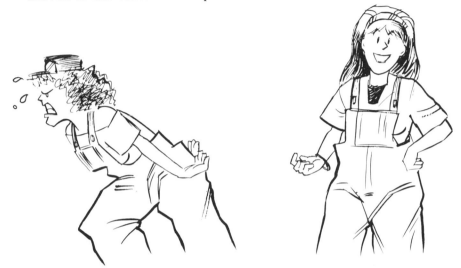

Raising Walls

Carla and Molly each take an armful of boards and set them down, one at a time, along the four lines of a square building (soon to be!). Working side by side, they lift a board and prepare to nail it in place.

Carla, hammer in hand, puts a handful of nails in her mouth. She takes one and carefully sets it exactly where she wants it. Molly get impatient. She slaps Carla on the back and points at the nail. *We're not nuclear physicists, you know! Just hammer the darn thing!*

Carla staggers backwards and gulps! The slap on the back caused her to swallow the nails! *I'm done! The nails will get stuck and I'll rust from the inside out!*

Molly waves her worries aside. She's got an idea. She grabs Carla by the heels and turns her upside down. With Carla balanced on her hands and head, Molly shakes her by the ankles. That finished, she lets Carla roll forward to a sitting position. Carla burps and spits out the regurgitated nails.

You're Nailed!

Getting back to business, they each take a handful of nails and begin hammering away. The walls begin to take shape, with one board after the next being nailed into place. Everything seems to be going just fine ... until Carla accidentally pounds a nail through her thumb.

HELP!

Molly jumps a foot in the air upon Carla's scream. *Hey, take it easy! I'll help you. But first, a little fun!* Molly grabs Carla's foot and tickles her toes! Not sure whether to laugh or cry, Carla tries to strike out at Molly. The nail in her thumb, however, prevents her from reaching very far. Molly stays just outside Carla's range and taunts her for a moment before changing moods. *Enough fun, okay? I'll get that nail out.*

Molly puts the hammer claw beneath Carla's thumb and pries up. *Boy! That's in tight! Rrrrgh!* After much pain and anguish, the nail comes out of the board—but not out of Carla's thumb! *No problem!* Molly grabs the thumb and pounds on the nail out with her hammer. *Good as new!*

Up on the Roof

With all four walls in place, Wally and Carla look up above at where the roof will be. Molly rubs her hungry stomach and yawns. *How about a break?*

Carla is genuinely disappointed in her co-worker's attitude. *Just because Rome wasn't built in a day doesn't mean this house won't be built in a day! You get the ladder, I'll get the lumber!*

Molly puts the ladder in place while Carla throws the lumber on top of the walls. Molly looks at the ladder and trembles slightly. She doesn't particularly *like* ladders. *Go on,* says Carla, *climb on up! Oh, alright! Hop on.*

Molly hops on Carla's back and shuts her eyes while Carla struggles to climb the ladder. This is apparently the only way Molly can overcome fear of ladders. Carla finally gets to the top and unloads Molly. Though exhausted from the climb, Carla immediately begins putting the roof together. Molly is more interested in the view, however, and leans forward to see more. She leans a little too far and begins frantically waving her arms to keep from falling off the edge. Carla grabs her by the belt loop and saves her. *Now quit fooling around and get to work!*

One board after another falls into place as Carla and Molly work furiously. Actually, Carla works furiously and Molly pretends to work furiously. Every time Carla turns her back, Molly yawns and stretches and checks out the view.

The Master's Touch

Molly gets on Carla's back again and they climb down the ladder. Molly smiles wide and wipes her hands. *All finished? Time to go home?*

Carla glowers at her and picks up two cans of paint. *Here, take one.* Molly shrugs, takes the can, and reluctantly begins painting the walls.

To make her task a little more enjoyable, she begins painting pretty pictures: flowers, birds, trees, and stars. *My, my! Isn't that the prettiest . . .* SPLAT! Carla comes along and quickly paints over the masterpiece. She doesn't have time for such foolishness!

Molly falls in line and begins painting the "right" way. Brush, brush, brush. Dip the brush in the paint can and brush, brush, wipe, wipe, smear, smear. Do it again. And again. *Isn't there a faster way? Maybe . . .* She tosses away the brush and throws the whole can of paint onto the wall. *Hey, that works great!* She grabs another can of paint and does the same with the second wall, and again with the third. *Finished!*

Carla, still busy with the first wall, looks up with disbelief. She checks each wall and sees that Molly has indeed put genuine effort into her work. She shakes her hand and pats her on the back. *I had you all wrong!*

Finished! For Good!

Molly takes advantage of Carla's happiness to press for some time off. *Let's go inside and take a nap!*

Carla starts to say no, but checks herself. *We're ahead of schedule. Why not?* She opens the door for Molly. *After you!* Molly enters and Carla follows. They're proud of their work. They look around at the walls and nod their heads with appreciation. *Not bad, not bad.*

Molly notices that the door is still open. She swings it shut and turns to Carla. Suddenly, the happiness leaves their faces. They

Oh dear!
Molly points to a side wall. It too falls over!
What's happening?!
They turn to the back wall. CRASH!
How can this be happening?
The fourth and final wall falls over.
Molly and Carla turn to each other as if to say, *What's a person supposed to do, huh?*
And then a look of pure terror crosses their faces. Very slowly, they look up at the ceiling . . .
The stage lights quickly fade to black.

Wally Says:

Some simple costume making is in order for this routine. Cut cardboard in 8" x 10" squares and paint them with the bright colors used on the popular Rubik's cube puzzle: green, yellow, red, blue, white, orange. Pin or strap these squares to your clothing (including a "cube" over your head!) so that you look like a puzzle come to life. Silly? You bet!

Cube's Rubik

The Puzzle

In the center of the stage sits a mass of tangled bodies. It looks like a giant, writhing *thing* out of a 1950's horror movie. Arms are wrapped over legs, heads seem to come out of feet, torsos curl over other torsos. It's difficult to determine how many different bodies comprise the mass. Four? Eight?

The Puzzled

Who should come walking by but the Puzzle Man. He stops and studies the tangled bodies for a second, then scratches his head. *What IS this? What's it doing here?* Unable to come up with any satisfactory answers, he resumes his merry walk and passes by the mass. But . . . something makes him stop.

The Joy of Puzzling

The Puzzle Man retraces his steps until he is once again standing in front of the bodies. He concentrates on it. He reaches forward and changes the position of one of the arms. Though the arm continues to wiggle and writhe, it doesn't move far from its basic position.

The Puzzle Man moves another arm, a leg, a head, and a couple of other body parts. He steps back and scratches his head again. The mass doesn't seem to look any different than it did a moment ago! He moves some more things around. No improvement. He holds his head in despair, then makes more changes.

AAARGH! He stomps his feet and shakes his arms. *This is frustrating! I can't figure this darn thing!*

Sufficiently stymied, he hauls off and kicks the human puzzle. It flies apart! One body rolls here, another rolls there, and another somewhere else.

The Solution

Ooops! The Puzzle Man steps back, embarrassed that his temper got the best of him. Or did it? He looks at the pieces and comes up with a brilliant idea. He runs here and grabs a body or two, brings them to the center of the stage, and stands them on their feet side by side. He runs over there and somewhere else, returning with all the bodies.

In a matter of seconds he completes (solves?) the puzzle. The human bodies stand shoulder to shoulder in a circle, hands linked, backs facing the center.

The Stickler

The Puzzle Man notices that one human is positioned backwards. *No big deal, just turn him around!* But when he turns him around, the two adjacent humans turn backwards!

Oh dear!

He turns one of them around (while holding the original backward-facing human firmly in position) and two others fall down in the center of the circle. Each correction in the puzzle only leads to further confusion for the poor Puzzle Man. In moments he has what he began with: a big blob of tangled humans. He shrugs his shoulders and walks off.

I give up! It's a stupid game, anyway! I've got better things to do.

Bubble Gum Swap

The Chewing Out

Wally walks into the store, chooses a piece of gum, and pays for it. He walks out with a big smile on his face and carefully unwraps the gum. He reads the tiny cartoon on the wrapper and throws it away. *Let's get down to business.*

He puts gum in his mouth and begins chewing. It must be an old piece because it's hard and dry. Wally strains his jaw and neck muscles to chew. He even uses his arms, pushing down on his head and up on his jaw.

Bubbling Forth

Eventually, the gum gets chewed. *Ah, nice and soft!* Wally shuts his eyes for a moment and savors the joy of chewing bubble gum. *What could be finer?*

He answers his own question and stops chewing and opens his eyes wide. *Of course!* He moves the gum forward in his mouth, takes a deep breath, and tries to blow a bubble. But the gum is still too hard. Wally's face turns red and his eyes get wide as his lungs try to expand the gum. No luck.

He chews some more, displaying signs of impatience. He blows again. This time, the gum flies out of his mouth and lands on the ground. Quickly looking over his shoulder to make sure no one is watching, he picks up the gum, brushes it clean, and puts it back to his mouth.

Blowing again, a huge bubble slowly emerges from his mouth.

Splat

The bubble explodes and Wally tumbles backwards. He sits up, slightly dazed, trying to figure out what happened.

Right then, his old friend Carla comes strolling along. She looks down at Wally and begins laughing. Wally doesn't see what's so funny. *What are you laughing at?*

Carla points at his face while continuing to chuckle. Wally

feels his chin and cheeks. *Yick! Gum all over my face!* He gets to his feet and narrows his eyes at Carla. *Alright, the fun's over!* She does her best to appear serious and concerned, but an occasional smile manages to break through.

A Sticky Subject

Wally slowly peels the gum off his face. Carla grimaces and appears somewhat disdainful. *Ugh. How crude!*

When Wally finally gets all the gum off, he rolls it into a tight ball and prepares to pop it back into his mouth . . . until he sees Carla's reaction. *How disgusting! How vile! How gross!* Although he doesn't like to be manipulated by Carla, Wally sees her point. Perhaps the gum *has* outlived its usefulness.

Gummed Up

Wally flicks his hand to throw the gum aside. *What the . . .?* He looks and sees that the gum is stuck to the palm of his hand. *Well, I'll be darned.* With Carla once again trying to repress a giggle, he flicks his hand more firmly. Still stuck. He flicks his hand rather *furiously!* That gum's not going anywhere. Wally tries to conceal his anger and embarrassment with a laugh and fails miserably.

He holds his hand out and, with the finger of his other hand, flicks at the gum. He looks up in the air but doesn't see it. The gum is stuck on the tip of his finger! Carla can no longer contain herself. She holds her sides while laughing at Wally.

Angered, Wally flicks at the gum with his other finger and meets the same success. Back and forth, finger to finger! His anger grows until suddenly, it dissolves into a smile. A sneaky smile. With the gum on the tip of his finger, he reaches forward and puts it on Carla's nose. Since she's laughing so hard he has to call it to her attention.

What are you talking about? I haven't got anything on my nose. I . . . ugh! Guhross!

Wally smiles quietly, contentedly and walks off, leaving Carla with the problem of how to dispose of the used bubble gum. After Wally disappears (and trying all the methods of removal that Wally tried), Carla swallows her pride, shuts her eyes, and . . . swallows the gum!

Entropy

In the Beginning . . .

Molly, Larry, and Carla are standing frozen in different poses. The angles of their bodies and arms are stiff and abrupt, for they are mechanical robots who are, at the moment, out of power.

Molly's arm jerks with a spasm of energy and then swings limp. Her upper body slowly bends down and stops. Her motor is just plain tuckered out.

And Along Comes Wally

Wally enters the stage, a veritable dynamo. He walks as you would expect a mechanized man to walk: rapidly, with tight, jerky movements. Even his head darts from side to side and up and down.

Wally walks across the stage and exits without acknowledging the existence of the others. A second later he comes back on. *Did I miss something? I think I missed something. Yes, look here, I did miss something.*

He sees Molly and begins walking circles around her, scratching his head. *Something is wrong. Something is wrong. Ah, here it is!*

He stops behind her and points to something on her back. He

then reaches forward and begins winding a giant key that is connected to her back! Around and around, tighter and tighter! He
grimaces as he executes the final turn. *There! All finished and ready
to go!*

But nothing happens. Molly remains frozen. Frustrated, Wally
gives her a light kick in the rear. BOING! She springs to life!

All for One, One for All

Molly is filled with an initial excess of power and moves like a
blur. She soon slows down and begins moving like Wally, in a
very mechanical way. They smile and turn to Larry and Carla.
Let's wind them up, too!

No sooner said than done, Larry and Carla joins Molly and
Wally in scurrying about the stage, enjoying their replenished
energy supply.

But what's this? Wally is moving slower and slower! He's worried! He points to the key on his back and . . . stops motionless!
Molly goes to his aid and quickly winds him back to life. Meanwhile, Larry has begun to slow down and Carla is walking in
tight little circles, apparently stuck in a dizzying pattern.

Wally goes to Larry's aid, and Molly unsticks Carla. *There!
Everything good as new! Oh dear! Not me!*

Molly begins slowing down! Carla turns to wind her, but she
slows down, too. They're both frozen, completely out of energy.
Wally decides to help, but he's slowing down! As he reaches for
Carla's key, he stops, motionless. Now only Larry is able to help
them!

Winding Down Towards . . .

Larry turns Wally's key. With each turn, Wally comes up with
just enough energy to make a turn on Carla's key. In moments,
everybody is running at full power . . . but only for moments.

Larry runs out of power and stops. Molly slows down and
stops. Carla gets trapped in making tight circles and slows down
to a stop. Wally sees all this and shakes his head. He walks to
Larry (but slowly, for he is losing energy, too), and gives him a
few small winds before stopping. Larry begins to move, but
sluggishly, for Wally didn't have time to put him at full strength.
Larry manages to give Carla a few winds before coming to a stop.

Carla reaches for Molly's key and . . . stops! She's out of energy!

But not all is lost. Carla slowly falls forward and crashes to the floor. When she does, she bumps Molly's key! Molly has some energy! She turns to Wally and moves towards him, reaching for his key. But she hasn't enough energy to make it more than half the distance. She stops.

And there the four of them are, still waiting for someone to come along and wind them up again.

Carla Says:

A real challenge! In this routine I'm a blob of clay that gets molded into a statue and then comes to life. The trick isn't so much coming to life (act natural when you do) as it is holding perfectly still while a statue (especially when the sculptor gets it into his mind to tickle you).

The Sculptor's Scene

The Sculptor's Scene

Woolly Wally sits at his table diligently working on a bottle of spirits. He's dressed in a tattered and dirty artist's smock. In the center of the floor lies a pile of burlap sacks and old blankets. Wally looks at the pile with resentment: *I wish it'd go away!* As if to show the pile how serious he is, he takes a long, hard swig from the bottle and slams it back down on the table. He shakes his head and sneers.

The Force Behind the Genius

Into the room rushes the sculptor's wife, Molly, looking worriedly for the source of the noise. She's a tired, haggard woman with no teeth, stiff joints, and a bit of a limp. Though she looks older than her years, she's no wiser. She loves her shiftless sculptor.

Wally slides the bottle beneath his smock as she approaches his table. He does a second-rate job of looking inconspicuous: head hangs low, eyes furtively dart from one edge of the table to the other, never looking up, teeth chew lip with rodent rapidity.

Molly stands over him and sadly shakes her head. *Wally, Wally, Wally . . . What are you doing sitting around?*

She rubs her stomach: *We're hungry.* She digs into her pockets and pulls them inside out: *We're broke. We need money. You've got to get to work, my poor, dear husband.* She points to the pile in middle of the floor and mimics the hammering of a chisel. She smiles and gives him a loving kiss.

The Artistic Flare

Wally, however, is in no mood to be fooled with the sweet routine. He doesn't like people bossing him around. He turns his face away from her kiss and roughly shoves her shoulder. *Knock it off! I'm my own boss! I'll do what I want to do and when I want to!*

He stand up and glowers over her, his fist poised to pound the point home. Molly is confused. How can someone she loves so much be so cruel? Undaunted, she smiles and holds her hands out to him. Wally takes a half-step back, pulls his arm to strike, and . . . the bottle drops out from beneath his smock.

Moods change quickly. Wally's anger deflates and is replaced with embarrassment, a bully caught with his pants down. Molly herself is chilled. Finding out that her husband is spending what little money they have on booze leaves her numb. She doesn't know what to do or say. Her problems are solved for her when Wally takes charge. He yells at her, roughly turns her around, and boots her out the door. *Get lost! How can I get anything done with you bothering me all day?*

Back to the Grind

Slamming the door shut, Wally stomps over to the pile of burlap sacks. He sighs deeply and rubs the back of his neck. *I guess I can't put it off any longer. Or wait! Maybe I can!* He picks up his bottle to have just a few more swigs. Empty! He tosses it aside. *It was worth a try.*

Leaning over the pile he scratches his head and tries to decide what to create. With his hands he outlines a shapely figure eight. He stares happily into an abyss. *A beautiful woman! Yes! Better than my tattered Molly!*

A Creative Act

He quickly tosses and kicks the burlap bags aside to reveal a mass of clay. (Which is actually Carla, in the act of portraying a mass of clay!). Reaching for one side, he pauses. *Maybe I should start over here . . . or here . . . or maybe . . . What the heck! I'll start here!*

His skilled fingers quickly shape the clay into something resembling a human torso. He lifts as he squeezes, and inch by inch the clay lengthens, ever upward. A little more tugging and more clay is now almost as tall as he is. He steps back to look. *Hmm.*

He tries to visualize long, slender legs out of twisted, bent clay. Delicate arms stretched out from a large lump on top. Maybe curl this clump back for a head. And of course . . . *I'll figure those out last.*

With the back of the sculpture facing the audience, Wally quickly and deftly gives shape to the legs, pulls out graceful arms, lifts a proud head, and . . . does last things last.

Finished!

Ah, how proud the artist is! He's done it again! Magnifique! He gently takes a stiff arm in two hands and turns the statue around, spinning it on its feet to face forward.

Is it not beautiful? he asks of no one and everyone. Looking into the eyes he sighs, allowing himself to be enchanted. His eyes continue to wander down the statue's body, a single finger tracing the gentle curves. *So beautiful, so sweet . . .*

Wally turns his head and looks at the door through which he booted his wife. He sneers. *So unlike that fly that buzzes about my life.*

Art Imitates Life

While looking at the door and dreaming his dreams, a hand sets lightly on Wally's shoulder. *Gulp!*

The statue is slowly coming alive. It's turning into Carla, Wally's dream incarnate. But Wally is afraid to move, fearful he might wake himself up. Carla's hand (and only her hand moves) slowly slides up his shoulder, onto his neck, then caresses his face.

Delightfully delirious, Wally turns and faces his creation. Joint by joint (just like the Tin Man!), Carla comes to life. No longer stiff and frozen, she's soft and supple and smiling into Wally's eyes. She puts a kiss on her fingertips and teasingly places it on his lips. Wally is numb with a kind of excitement he hasn't experienced in years. Overcome, he stands numb and mute while Carla, every bit the enchantress, dances circles around him, slipping her hands over his fat tummy, ruffling his hair, running her fingers across his face.

Senses Regained

Every man has his limit, even Wally. He makes a grab for Carla. She evades him and laughs. *Care to try again?* You bet! Again and again Wally tries to embrace her, each time failing, each time getting more and more excited. He puts his hand on his heart: *I love you, Carla, I want only you.*

She comes towards him with her hands held up to stop his energetic advances. *Patience. I'm yours now. There's no hurry.* They embrace. He bends to kiss her . . .

. . . When Molly comes in.

A Private Gallery

More surprised than embarrassed, Wally jumps back and licks his lips, rapidly thinking of something to say. Molly looks at him with kindness and a bit of confusion. *What's the problem?* All she sees is a statue, frozen in a rather awkward position. Wally looks at the statue, too. He smiles and winks at it, as if sharing a secret: *That's a good trick, baby. Stay that way until I take care of things.*

Molly walks over and admires the statue. Very beautiful. Wally steps between her and the statue. He puts his arm over it and points at his chest with his thumb. *It's mine! It's all I want, and that means I don't want you. Go!* He turns and winks again at the statue.

Meanwhile, Molly gives Wally a peck on the cheek and smiles. *Of course. I don't want to disturb your work.* She points to her watch to indicate when she'll return.

Good old Wally laughs at her ignorance. He grabs her arm and rips the watch off and throws it away. *When I say go, I mean scram!* He storms over to the closet, pulls out two travel bags, quickly shoves some of her clothes into them, and drops them at Molly's feet. He points to the door and raises his fist.

Poor Molly is horrified. She could live with the fact that her husband was something of a loser as long as she knew he loved her (in his own way). But this . . . ! Her world was being turned upside down!

Wally works the knuckles of his fist and begins counting. One . . . two . . . three . . . Molly wipes away the tears, grabs her bags, and makes for the door. Before leaving she turns and gives him a final smile.

Back to the Drawing Board

With Molly good and gone, Wally rushes back to embrace his lovely Carla. He giggles. *Now, where were we?*

He steps back. Something's not right. Carla remains a frozen statue. He snaps his fingers. *She's gone! No need to worry! We're safe!* Nothing. He shakes the statue with no better luck. To make things worse, the statue begins melting. The arms flop inward, the head sags, the back curves, the knees collapse . . . and a pile of unshapen clay rests at his feet.

What have I done? Was I dreaming? Am I dreaming still?

Shaken, he looks to the door. *Molly!* He runs to the door, opens it, and looks for his banished wife. She too is gone.

What now?

He slowly picks up the bottle he had earlier tossed aside. He turns it upside down and waits for a drop to fall on his tongue. When nothing happens he sticks his finger inside to wipe off any lingering moisture . . . and finds that he can't remove his finger. He's stuck with himself between a blob of clay and a forsaken woman.

Molly Says:

Not much of a plot in this routine, but who cares? Kids don't, anyway, and they're the audience you'll most likely be performing this one for. Have fun!

The Silly Circus

Presenting . . .

The Master of Ceremonies for the Silly Circus (Larry, who else?) enters the center ring in a grand, proud strut. He readjusts his high top hat, twirls the ends of his monstrous handlebar moustache, and taps his swagger stick in the palm of his open hand. He waves his arms and grandly proclaims that the Silly Circus has begun!

He picks up a title card and points to Ring One: MADCAP MONKEYS! He bows and quietly exits while the monkeys (Molly, Carla, and Wally) enter.

Many Monkeys

Looking like they just fell out of the tree, the monkeys come bouncing out to the center of the ring and line up side by side. They do a pretty good job of imitating monkeys, too. (Not that it's very difficult for this bunch of mimes to act like monkeys!) Sitting on their haunches they scratch their sides and move their arms and hands and heads in quick, nervous movements. Wally leans over to bite a tick out of Carla's neck, but she won't have anything to do with it. She whacks him on the head and bares her teeth.

Molly slaps the floor. *Time for our first trick.*

Wally covers his ears. Carla covers her eyes. Molly (as one might guess) covers her mouth. Trick finished, the monkeys roll somersaults, laugh, bounce up and down, and congratulate each other on the hilarity of their stunt. Somewhere in the middle of the fracas, Wally peels a banana, eats it, and drops the peel.

The Master of Ceremonies enters hurriedly and claps, more for the purpose of getting the monkeys to leave than to applaud. Larry happens to step on the banana peel and falls very unceremoniously (especially for a Master of Ceremonies) on his tail end. The monkeys never knew anything could be so funny and laugh their way away.

Delightful Doggies

After regaining his composure, Larry holds the next title card: DOGGIE DOINGS. He leaves as the dogs (again, Molly, Wally, and Carla) take the spotlight.

They prance about, wagging their tails, panting, and letting their tongues hang low. Like most dogs, they are happy and seemingly good-natured. After making a complete tour of the stage, they begin their tricks.

First, they all sit up on their hind legs. Wally looks at the audience like something is wrong. He claps his hands and urges the audience to do likewise. *Come on and cheer! This may look easy, but it's hard work!*

For the second trick they stand on their hind feet and turn pirouettes. Molly has a little problem with this one and falls over, knocking the other two dogs to the floor. They scramble back to their original line-up and prepare for trick number three, which is nothing more than rolling over and playing dead. Again Wally has to encourage the audience to applaud. Having finished the routine, they prance merrily away.

Big Gray

Larry, M of C, returns with another title card: BIG GRAY.

Big Gray turns out to be none other than Wally the Elephant and his trainer, Carla. She sits atop his back as he slowly shuffles forward on all fours. What's everybody laughing at? Why, probably that short length of green hose attached over his face with duct tape! A pretty silly excuse for an elephant's trunk, but what do you expect from the Silly Circus?

Carla dismounts (and Wally sighs happily!) and moves with the exaggerated theatrics of a circus performer. *Trick One . . .* She claps her hands in front of Wally's face. He rears back and lifts his two front feet. Carla quickly gets to her knees and places her head on the ground, directly beneath the elephant's feet. *How about that! Courting death! At the very least a severe migraine!*

After crawling back to her feet, she announces the next trick. *Hup!* The elephant rolls his eyes. He doesn't like this trick. Carla holds out three fingers. The elephant, with his front leg, pounds the floor three times. As Carla turns to the audience to receive her well-earned applause, the elephant (as though he doesn't know what he's doing!) stomps his foot a fourth time. Carla gives him a dirty look and moves on to the next trick. *Roll over! Roll over!*

You can't say that the elephant doesn't give it his best shot. But try as he might, he gets stuck on his back and can't get to his feet. Carla scowls. *I said to roll over! Hurry up, this is embarrassing!* In the end, she has to help him complete the roll. They bow for their applause and prepare to leave. Carla climbs atop the elephant's back and . . . woof! The elephant collapses under the weight. Again Carla has to help him to his feet. She leads him off by pulling his silly green trunk.

Follow-up Act

The Master of Ceremonies steps out and tries to build applause for the elephant act. It's clear he finds the quality a bit below par, but that doesn't stop him from exhorting the audience. *What's that? I can't hear you? Ah, that's better.* The color suddenly leaves his face. He looks down at his foot. *Oops. I'm stepping where a big elephant's been!* He motions to a laborer, Molly, who hustles out with a shovel and does some traditional post-elephant cleaning. Larry is pleased and gives her his own applause. *Much better, thank you!*

He turns to the audience. *On with the show!* The new title card reads: LION TAMER!

Lion Tamer Tamed

Wally backs out onto the stage. He's one busy lion tamer. He holds a chair in one hand and is busy cracking a bullwhip with the other. He moves to the center and directs the lion (as yet invisible) to the other side. *That's where I want you! Now stay!*

(LION TAMER SWITCHES TO LION)

The lion is in a sitting position staring at his tamer. He snarls and roars and waves a menacing paw with fangs extended. *I'm King of the Forest! Nobody tells me what to do!* Cuh-rack! The whip snaps above his head and he winces. *Nobody but for guys with whips . . .*

To vent his anger, he bellows forth with a mighty roar.

(SWITCH TO LION TAMER)

The lion tamer grabs his ears and squirms with pain! *Can that kitty yell or what?* He recovers and quickly moves on to his series of tricks. The whip cracks as the tamer guides the lion around in a circle, then prompts him to leap on top of a pedestal. If that's not enough, he gets the lion to leap through the air from one pedestal to another! He turns and bows for a big round of applause.

(SWITCH TO LION)

This may be fun for humans, but it's humiliating for proud lions to go prancing about. The lion takes a moment to clean his claws. When he looks up at the tamer he can't help but lick his lips.

(SWITCH TO TAMER)

The tamer holds his hands high for quiet. Time for the big trick. He snaps his whip and moves in close to the lion. He moves carefully and slowly. He reaches for the lion's head and slowly opens the jaws. *Drum roll, please.* Sticking his head between the jaws, he smiles and waves for applause.

(SWITCH TO LION)

The lion is sitting with his mouth open wide, surrounding a human head. He looks to the audience, raises his eyebrows, smiles, and . . . chomps down. *Mmmm!* He chomps again and swallows. Chomp, chomp, chomp. Swallow, swallow, swallow. He looks down, picks some tiny piece up from the floor, swallows it, licks his lips, and casually walks away.

The Master of Ceremonies nervously rushes out with another title card: VANISHING ACT!

He waves and runs away, followed by the lion.

Larry Says:

You can stick this routine some- where in the middle of The Silly Circus, but I prefer to perform it separately. Pay special attention to developing tension in the au- dience's eyes as you balance precariously. You might even pick up some pointers by watch- ing a slack-rope (usually a rope with no tension strung between two points, dangling a foot or two above the ground) walker, or giving it a try yourself!

Highwire

One Step at a Time

Ta-dum! Larry and Carla, highwire artists extraordinaire, prance nobly to the center of the stage, join hands, and take a deep, theatrical bow. Looking up, up, up, and up, they raise their hands and point to the highwire. *Time for the show to begin!*

Larry and Carla unclasp their capes at the shoulder and hand them to assistants. With a good luck handshake, they part and head for opposite sides of the stage and the ladders that lead up to the highwire. Carla quickly begins climbing with a tireless ease. Larry sighs and reluctantly grabs hold of a rung. *I'm not so sure this is my idea of a fun evening . . .*

Marathon Runging

Hand over hand, foot after foot, rung after rung, Larry plods onward . . . er, upward. The novelty soon wears off to be re- placed with a genuine boredom. He looks over at Carla and sneers. She's climbing as though no other endeavor could be more fulfilling. Larry shakes his head. *I prefer excitement. Endurance is for the birds. Ooops!*

Larry's hand slips and he falls down the length of the ladder, frantically reaching out to grab it. His arms flail and his legs wave (in a speed somewhere between slow-motion and normal). With one desperate lunge he manages to grab a rung. His fall comes to an abrupt (and painful) halt as his body swings forward and slams into the ladder. He rubs his nose, shakes his head clear, and resumes his climb, this time with a bit more concentration. He quickly scampers to the top of the ladder. *Whew!* Across from him, on the platform at the other end of the highwire, waits an impatient Carla.

How High Is High?

Larry waves to Carla and leans forward on his knees to catch his breath . . . and almost dies of a heart attack! *YIKES! HELP! What am I doing way, way, WAY up here?!* Larry promptly begins to go a little bit insane. He shakes, draws his knees together, and looks around him with a glazed gaze.

Meanwhile, who should join Larry but good old Wally. He flies in on the trapeze, lands with a plop, loses his grip, and watches the trapeze drift away. *Darn! Well, there's more where that came from.*

Wally gets to his feet and sees Larry. After a hearty laugh he slaps Larry on the back. *Come on, buddy, you got a show to give! How about it? Go on, get out there!*

Larry gives tentative signs of compliance.

No-Frills Chills and Thrills!

Carla, with a flamboyant, confident wave of the arms, steps lightly onto the wire. With minor (but noticeable) checks on balance, Carla executes a series of death-defying, crowd-catering maneuvers. She stands on one foot, bends down to her knee, does a somersault, skips rope, juggles and even files her nails! She looks over at Larry. *Anytime, partner.*

Wally gives the guy a shove. *Go on, what's there to be afraid of?*

Larry timidly steps forth and sets his foot on the wire. He wipes the sweat from his brow and tries to control his shaking. Another step. He licks his lip. His eyelids flutter. Another step.

And another. Before he knows it he's standing in the middle of the wire (in the middle of the stratosphere).

He looks down and nervously laughs. *Ha, aah, ha ha! I guess it wasn't so hard after all!*

The power of the mind to deceive the body is truly an amazing thing. Carla, now standing next to Larry, reaches out and taps him on his shoulder. Nervously clearing her throat, she points to the wire. *Er, excuse me, uh, maybe this isn't quite the right moment to tell you this, but, uh, the wire is over here. You're sort of in kind of the wrong place in space.*

Larry examines the wire. He points to the wire and nods his head. *Ah, yes, so I am in the wrong place. Hmm. Hmm? HELP!* Looking something like the befuddled Coyote in a *Road Runner* cartoon, he scrambles on air and manages to make his way back to the wire. Carla grabs hm and tries to steady him, but it's a difficult task. The wire is bouncing and swaying and Larry is clawing and grasping her for security. She pushes him away and quickly

makes her way to her platform. She grabs a trapeze, looks back at Larry, and rolls her eyes, then flies away.

This Wire Is Wired!

Wally finds this entire escapade quite amusing. He can't help but get into it. With a merry jaunt, he hops out on the wire beside Larry. *Fun, huh buddy? No? Well, how about this?* Wally starts hopping up and down on the wire, shaking it, swaying it back and forth, and all kinds of things, all designed specifically to give Larry the ride of his life. Unable to hang on any longer, Larry plummets. Wally chortles and scurries back to his platform to watch the descent.

Down Is a Long Way

Sheer horror covers Larry's face. This time there's no ladder to reach out and grab. There's only time for . . . prayer! But no sooner does he begin apologizing for his sins (which should take him an hour or so) than he hits the safety net! *Booooiiiinnnggg! Boooiiinngg! Booiing! Boing!*

He jumps off the net and kisses the solid earth. *Greatest thing ever invented!* But his happiness is not so great as to blind his anger. He looks up at Wally, who is pointing down at Larry and trying to control his laughter. *What a sucker!*

Bouncing Back

Larry goes to the corner of the safety net, pulls out a knife, and cuts it loose. He repeats the process until the net has completely fallen. Putting the knife between his teeth, he quickly, fearlessly, determinedly ascends the ladder opposite Wally.

Wally laughs. *Oh, I'm scared alright. See me shake? Huh?* Wally prances out on the wire and waits for Larry, who soon joins him.

Larry pulls the knife out of his mouth. *Take this, Mr. Practical T. Joker!* With a quick slash, Larry cuts the wire apart between Wally's feet!

Wally's not laughing anymore. He reaches down and grabs the two ends to prevent himself (the heck with Larry!) from falling down to a safety netless earth. *What do you think you're doing, anyway?* Larry thinks he's flying away on the trapeze and promptly does so, leaving Wally to hang around. Wally slips and is now hanging below the wire. He casts a threatening glance at the audience. *If I hear one joke about coming unwired . . .*

Molly Says:

A few costumes are quite helpful for making identification of the monsters a bit easier (and more visually entertaining) for the audience.

Monster Mess

Tobacco Proven Superior to Garlic

Molly fusses about the bedroom preparing for her night's journey through the land of sleep, via a one-seat bed. It's a wonder she can see, though, what with all the cigarette smoke! She's got a cigarette in each hand and puffs on them alternately, one deep drag after another. You'd think she was afraid of suffocating on oxygen.

She readies her bed: pulls back the covers, brushes out bits of dirt, lint, bugs, whatnot, fluffs the pillow. She turns and opens her closet, takes off her clothes, and selects an appropriate bed gown.

Meanwhile . . .

Who should poke his nose through the window but the dashing darkly handsome Count Dracula? He sniffs the air, spots Molly, and smiles his lascivious, liqueous leer.

Molly doesn't notice him, of course, and goes right on preparing for bed, smoking, and lighting a few new cigarettes to replace the spent stubs. She walks over to her dresser and takes a seat in front of the mirror. Primp time. As she begins brushing her hair, the smooth Count begins creeping forward with all the grace of an old-time movie vampire: lots of flourishes with the cape, waving of hands, bending and curling of fingers.

Molly stops long enough to catch up on her smoking. She rapidly puffs on two or three cigarettes. *Ah, that feels good!* The Count is now poised above her. He licks his lips, coils his fingers, and descends upon the back of her neck. His lips curl back revealing hungry teeth. Molly, busy puffing away, doesn't notice the Count. She can't see him in the mirror and she can't feel his teeth sink into her flesh. No, she's too preoccupied with smoking to notice much of anything around her. Just as Dracula can't get enough of her blood (When's he going to come up for air, anyway?), Molly can't get enough tobacco.

Finally, the Count disengages himself from the back of Molly's neck. He turns to the audience. What's this?! The Count isn't pleased with a healthy (relatively speaking) quaffing at the stream of life? A sickly pallor (again, relatively speaking) comes over his face as he grabs at his throat. He suddenly begins choking violently, gasping for air and holding his chest. Did he miss the artery and tap into a smoke filled windpipe?

Molly finally notices him. *Poor guy. Here, have a cigarette.* Dracula draws back in horror. He holds his hands up and crosses his index fingers to form a crucifix. *Protect me from this anathema!* He backs offstage, unable to shake that hacking cough.

Wraparound Love Affair

Molly dismisses the vampire with a wave of her hand. *I've got more important things to do. Curl my hair, for instance. Yes, that's what I'll do!*

With Count Dracula good and gone, Molly loses her interest in smoking. She returns to her mirror and devotes full attention to the curling of her hair, winding one curler after another and occasionally brushing out a rat or two.

Perhaps his olfactory senses are deteriorating with age, but it seems a certain mummy has mistaken the clouds of tobacco smoke for the smoke from the nine sacred tanna leaves. He pokes his head in the room and sniffs. *Yes, this is the sacred temple!* The mummy shuffles into the room as only mummies can: his arms held out stiff, left leg dragging, neck and head locked permanently in one position. How do we know he's a mummy? He's wrapped in reams of toilet paper! (and he's wrapped very carefully, as we shall soon discover).

He moves forward. *Ah! The Holy Priestess! Preparing for our wed-*

ding! His hands waver before him with desire, his fingers itch and curl. (After all, the guy's been waiting a few thousand years for this day.) Standing over Molly, he prepares to take her in his arms.

The Passion Unwinds

Molly could give a hoot about sacred weddings. What's bothering her at the moment is the greasy cold cream on her face. She pokes at it with her fingers. *Yicky poo!* She begins to wipe the goop away with her fingers but thinks better of it. *Why mess up my hands? I'll use one of these tissues instead.*

She reaches behind and grabs a loose strand of toilet paper off the mummy. She pulls . . . and the mummy begins spinning! Unwinding! Molly pulls more and more (she wants to be very clean) and the mummy continues to unwind, stumbling backward and offstage. His only legacy to his beloved is a mountain of crumpled toilet paper.

Lycanthropus Lechurus

Molly looks at herself in the mirror. *There! All good and squeeky clean!* Is she finally finished with her seemingly endless toilette? Hardly. She scratches her knee and can't help but notice a rough stubble of hair. She searches and finds that the stubble extends from her ankles to her . . . to well above her knees. *Better do something about that.*

While Molly digs around for a razor, yet another visitor pays a call. Who else but *C. Lycanthropus*, a.k.a. the werewolf? He crawls forward on all fours, sniffing the air, extending his claws and snarling. When Molly finds a straight-edge razor and begins sharpening it on a leather strap, the werewolf howls and licks his lips. *A werewolf has got to do what a werewolf has got to do.*

Another Close Shave

The werewolf slinks ahead until his nose is but inches from Molly's thigh. He opens his mouth to bite, but stops when Molly turns on him with a reproachful glare. *Can't you see I'm busy!* The werewolf shuts his mouth befuddled, uncertain, wondering why Molly isn't frightened to death.

Molly isn't befuddled. She's a woman of action. On closer inspection she finds that her stubble is nothing compared to the werewolf's hirsute mug. *Let me tidy you up a bit!* With but a few deft strokes of the straight edge, Molly gives the werewolf a face as smooth as a baby's bottom. The werewolf, now in an advanced state of bewilderment, rubs his face with the back of his paw. *Aaargh! How am I ever going to scare anyone now!?*

He turns on Molly with renewed, genuine anger. She's not exactly shaken. Actually, she's miffed that he doesn't appreciate her barbering skills. *Growl at me, will you? Well, take this!* She rolls up a newspaper, swats him on the tail end, and chases him out of the room!. *Scram, you grateless lycanthrope!*

Time to Hit the Sheets

Tired of visitors, tired of preparing for bed . . . just plain tired, Molly heads for bed. She yawns, stretches, and climbs beneath the sheets. The stage lights fade slowly to black. As the lights near total blackness, something strange begins to happen, something that maybe only a careful viewer will notice. The sheets begin to rise and hover! They move away from the bed, ghostlike, leaving an empty spot where Molly only moments ago reclined. They vanish offstage.

Carla Says:

More snappy little bits to change the rhythm of the show. The second routine is mostly a showcase for your technical skills. It'll take the audience a moment to slow down with you and appreciate what you're doing, so don't worry if they're a little fidgety at first.

Hot Stuff

Rockin' Wally and the Accomplices (Carla the Cutter and Larry Lust) charge out onto the stage like they're looking for a fight. Not finding one, they pick up their instruments and launch into an energy packed heavy metal rock performance. This is one mean, tough band. The Pentagon could learn lessons from this bunch on how to use music as a weapon.

Rockin' Wally is the lead singer. He screams into his microphone, not to mention spits, stomps, and slugs the mike. He waves it menacingly at the audience and his partners on stage. He slings the microphone cord like a whip, smashing his feet to the floor and kicking at the phantoms in the air.

Larry Lust, lead guitarist, uses his guitar alternately as a sword and machine gun. Occasionally, if only to make some noise, he cranks out a few hot licks. He duels momentarily with Rockin' Wally, cuts him in half, and turns away victorious. Rockin' Wally feigns death, then springs back to life with more vitriolic fervor than ever before.

Larry Lust now attacks Carla the Cutter. This requires a more strategic offensive charge as Carla is surrounded by her drums. Larry uses his guitar as a machine gun and Carla the drumsticks as six-shooters. They dodge back and forth behind the drums, shooting, hiding, and shooting again, all the time playing their instruments and keeping time. Rockin' Wally steps in just in time, cracks the whip, and separates the duel. Back to the music!

Dig it! They are hot stuff!

A Chilling Chord

Gramma Molly quietly enters the stage and trods along, struggling to lift her feet and clinging to her cane. Her back is bent, her mouth tight and drawn. As she passes in front of Rockin' Wally and the Accomplices, she stops and stares. Although they notice her, they continue their antics. Still, they seem distracted and anxious for her to move on. After all, this is *their* show. But

Gramma Molly is in no hurry. No, it seems the band is the object of her full attention and amusement.

Amusement? You bet! While watching Rockin' Wally gyrate and do strange things to his microphone she can't help but titter. *Oh dear! This reminds me of the Marx Brothers!* Wally finds it more comfortable to wander off to a neutral corner and let Gramma Molly watch someone else, namely, Carla the Cutter. The titter now becomes a giggle! *Isn't she the silliest thing trying to play those drums! She's funnier than Lucy Arnaz ever was!* Carla finds herself sheepishly hiding behind a drum.

Gramma Molly now turns to Larry Lust. She can't constrain herself any longer from breaking forth with peals of laughter. *Look at that boy! Oh, but Jerry Lewis should be so funny!* She totters offstage holding her chest and trying to stop from laughing (if only to catch her breath).

Meanwhile, the members of the band have quit playing. They stare at each other with reluctant embarrassment. Rockin' Wally does his best and starts singing, but the magic is gone. He gives up, shrugs his shoulders, and looks at the others. They sheepishly shrug their shoulders, drop their instruments, and walk offstage, carefully managing to avoid eye contact.

Slo-Mo Replay

Ready, Set, Hike!

It's the big game! And this is the big play! You can see it all in slow motion replay. Very, very slow motion. We pick up the action on the hike.

Larry is quarterback, Molly the center. On defense, Wally plays the line and Carla plays deep safety. The ball is snapped . . . as snappy as a slow motion replay can be. Everything and everybody moves slow, slow, slow. The ball seems to take forever to get into the quarterback's hands. When he does get it, he slowly backpeddles, lifts his head, and looks downfield.

Molly knocks Wally down and charges forward. Wally makes the most out of his big fall. He tumbles and crumples and slides his face through the dirt. Not seeming to be phased, he rolls back to his feet and chases after Larry.

Covered!

It appears to Carla that Molly is the intended pass receiver. She runs to meet her. Molly tries every trick in the book but can't shake Carla. Frustration is evident on Molly's face, determination on Carla's. Unable to bear it any longer, Molly grabs for Carla's facemask and twists her painfully to the ground. She laughs and takes off running . . . or tries to, as Carla grabs her ankle.

Scrambling!

This tight coverage on the pass receivers sends quarterback Larry scrambling for his life. It seems as though Wally's only purpose in life is to obliterate the existence of quarterbacks. He chases Larry to the left, then to the right, but each time Larry manages a deft twist of direction and evades Wally's clutches. Wally's pursuit is incredible, however, and he is now directly behind Larry. Cleverly, Larry puts on the brakes and Wally tumbles over him, again crashing to the ground.

Fumblings About

But what's this? Was Larry so clever he forgot to hold onto the football?! It bounces here and there (as only footballs can), continually going the direction Larry, and now Wally, are not. Quite the comical highlight of this slow motion replay!

Larry somehow manages to grab the ball . . . at the same moment Wally grabs him! Larry throws to Molly! The ball flies (floats) through the air. All eyes are on it. Up, up, and up it goes, slowly moving forward. If you didn't know this routine was in slow motion, you'd swear they were watching a cloud. Molly struggles free of Carla's grasp and begins to move in the direction of the ball. *How long is this going to take, anyway?* She motions impatiently with her hands.

A Step Above

One person who isn't going to wait any longer is Wally. He takes matters into his own hands by scrambling to the sidelines and returning with a long, cumbersome object: a ladder! He unfolds it and climbs to the top, just in time to steal the pass. The other players are in frozen shock as they watch him climb down and run for a touchdown.

Larry Says:

It's highly effective if you have control over lighting in this routine. Divide the stage into three distinct areas (two sides and a middle) with lights. Each area should have separate controls. Like the suggestions for most of the other routines, it's not a necessary requirement, but a helpful idea that should be employed when possible.

Dreams for the Dreaming

Spitter Spatter

Wally has his back turned on Molly not only because he's busy brushing his teeth, but also because he's not too interested in his wife. He tries to dismiss her by waving his hand over the back of his shoulder. *Yak, yak, yak! Get off my back!*

Molly throws her hands up in disgust, shakes her head, and goes back to prattling. She's mildly upset about something and can't quit talking about it. She goes through the motions of complaining very naturally, as though she's been doing it a long time. Tightening her robe and adjusting her glasses, she begins wagging a finger. Is she scolding her husband.

Wally gargles, spits, and heads for bed. He finally pauses and glances at Molly. He rolls his eyes and makes a gesture with his lips that says: *This is what I married? A chubby, over-the-hill chatterbox? Ech! Faster to sleep the better!* He lies down in bed and pulls the sheet (a real sheet, not imaginary) over his head to better exclude Molly from his senses.

Molly stops in mid-sentence. She sadly shakes her head. *Some husband. Doesn't care what I think, doesn't even pretend to listen.* Deflated, and with a certain resignation to her fate, Molly takes her robe off and climbs under the sheets. The lights on the right and left side of the stage go off, leaving only a center light over the bed.

Trucetime on the Marital Conference Table?

They are silent and still with their backs turned to each other. Things remain this way until finally Wally sits up and looks down at his wife. He rubs his hands together and smiles a mischievous smile. He's ready for a little nighttime recreation! *Oh darling!?* With a tippy tap on her shoulder he tries to rouse Molly's interest. He succeeds in rousing something, but definitely not what he wanted.

Yak, yak, yak, yakkity yak! Having pent up her tongue for over two minutes, Molly resumes her complaining with renewed energy. *Not to mention the yakkity yak with the yak yakker!*

Wally clamps his hands over his ears and buries his head in the pillow. *Gimme a break, would you? Just a little break?*

But no. It's more yak yak. If fades away when Molly looks down and sees that Wally is no longer listening. She sighs sadly. *We used to talk when we went to bed. We also used to . . .* Reminded of the past, Molly lovingly runs her hand up and down his side. *Remember?* She rubs some more. Wally is motionless. A little bit more and still no response. *DON'T YOU REMEMBER?!* Wally rolls around, yawns and is fast asleep. Her anger and frustration spent, Molly shrugs lightly and joins her husband in sleep.

The lights dim to total blackness.

Dream #1

The lights on Wally's side (let's say the right) of the stage slowly fade up to a low level, with Wally on the very edge.

Hmm? What? Waly tries to shake the cotton from his head. He yawns and stretches. *Time for work? Say, where the devil am I, anyway?* He notices the circle of light, sits up and bends forward to investigate. As he does, a Lilith-like apparition (in the form of Carla) moves towards him. His mouth drops open with amazement. *She's beautiful! And she's not yakking about anything, either!*

She stands over Wally and plays with his hair and ears. Wally's mouth drops open. He's in ecstasy! He's so far gone he has to shovel his tongue back in his mouth. The apparition now takes Wally's hand and pulls him to his feet. Doing her best to allure and entice him, she moves in soft, sinuous circles, always keeping her hands on his chest, neck or head. She whispers something into his ear. Wally thinks: *Sounds good to me!* She whispers into the other ear. *That sounds even better!*

With Wally nodding his head in the affirmative, Carla takes his hand, faces him, and backs away, leading him off the stage and away from his bed. At the edge of the light Wally puts on the brakes. He tries to explain: *Gee, I'd like to, honest, but . . .* Wally reluctantly looks back at his bed . . . and wife. He sighs. *I'm sorta stuck with her.* He smiles. *But you know, I sorta of like being stuck with her, too.*

Carla stomps her foot in fury, walks to the front center of the stage, and sits down, just out of the light. Wally meekly waves goodby. *Thank you, though, thank you . . . very, very much.* He sighs and crawls back in bed.

The lights fade out. In a moment, the lights on Molly's side fade up to a low level.

Dream #2

Molly jumps up with a start and begins yakking. What's going on? What are these lights doing . . . And sees an apparition (in the form of Larry) of her own. *Oh dear!* She turns to Wally for advice, *but he never pays attention, anyway. I'll take care of this myself!* There may be other reasons for her wanting to handle the situation on her own, reasons that can be seen in her most charming smile.

She stands, puts her robe on, and begins tightening it when Larry slowly and smoothly unties it and slips it off her shoulders. *Now listen, I don't . . .* Larry takes hold of her wagging finger and gently kisses it. Molly blushes. She likes this! She likes it so much she lets Larry put his arm around her and slowly escort her away from the bed. He's quite the charmer, and she's quite the charmee! She begins to tell him how nice and surprising this is to her. Larry listens patiently, even with interest.

Suddenly, at the edge of the light, Molly stops talking and freezes in her tracks. *What am I doing?! And what are you doing to me?!*

Larry gestures: *Er, nothing . . . unnatural.*

Molly looks back at the bed and starts yakking again. *But I can't go with you, I've got Wally, for better or worse, and if I leave him I just . . .*

Larry throws up his arms in depair and turns his back. Molly jabbers all the way back to the bed! After she's under the covers Larry walks across the front of the stage and almost trips over Carla. She jumps up, startled, and faces Larry. Both stand in the low light with sad faces. Larry looks into Carla's eyes. *Say, you're kind of pretty . . . for a dream!*

Carla smiles. *You're not so bad yourself!* They join arms and walk away.

Waking Up to a New Dream

The lights fade up to full brightness as Larry and Carla leave the stage. Wally sits up with a start and shakes his head. *Where am I? Am I back?* He turns to his wife and loses his startled look, replacing it with a tender smile. He pats her gently on the shoulder and she wakes up, yakking before completely conscious. Wally listens carefully, nodding and raising his eyebrows with appropriate interest. Molly stops and claps her hand over her mouth. *Oh dear! I'm yakking too much, aren't I?* Wally says he doesn't mind.

Molly doesn't care what he thinks, she's through talking and that's that. She zips her lip and throws away the key, then puts her arms around her husband. He's surprised. *Hm? Huh? What? Ohhhh . . .*

They pull the sheets over their heads and begin kicking about. The lights fade to darkness.

Happy Jack Says:

The following is a dramatized account of how I got to the end of this book. No names have been changed to protect the guilty.

Written Off

What's the Hurry?

Toward the front corner on the extreme right side of the stage sits a chair and small work table. Who should enter from the left but Happy Jack (yours truly), a special guest mime. He spots the tables and sneers. *When are you going to leave me alone?* Slowly, reluctantly, he makes his way to the table. He sneers again. *I really don't want to do this . . .* But with great inner effort he slides the chair back and plops himself down. *Here we go again.*

On the table in front of him is a typewriter, which Happy Jack prepares for use. He pulls a sheet of paper from a stack, sticks it in, centers it, and prepares to Create. This is done by cracking the knuckles of the fingers, stretching them, and then wiggling each one independently. Following with a deep breath he puts his fingers to the keyboard and . . . nothing.

His fingers are frozen. He panics. What's happening? Writer's block? Laziness? Mystic visions? Shaking his head he repeats the knuckle cracking routine. This time his fingers begin pecking away.

Hey?! What's going on here? The typewriter isn't working. Happy Jack raises a threatening fist and sees, out of the corner of his eye, that the machine isn't plugged in. He reaches down and puts the plug in place, grumbling. *The more gimmicks they add, the more that goes wrong. Just when I was on a roll, too!*

After another round of knuckle cracking he begins typing in earnest, his eyes and head following the carriage back and forth.

Back in the Box

As can happen only in the world of mime, Happy Jack types a character right onto the stage! Molly, to be precise. Whenever Happy Jack types, Molly obeys the commands of the letters and words, but when he pauses and reflects, Molly is free to express her own opinions and, to some extent, create her own actions.

Happy Jack smiles as he leads Molly along. Molly smiles too. She's having a good time. Now Happy Jack chuckles and Molly crashes into an invisible wall! Ouch! She's standing in the rear center of the stage (so that Happy Jack can turn his head occasionally and coordinate typing action with mime action).

Molly rubs her nose and takes a step back—into another wall! Panicky, she rushes forward and backward only to find a ceiling inches above her head. What a fix! She can only take a few steps in any one direction.

Happy Jack pauses to ruminate. Molly is now free. (Not free of the box, but of control over her actions.) She turns to Happy Jack and tries (but doesn't quite succeed) to smile goodnaturedly. *Alright, you've had you're fun. Now get me the *!#*! out of here!*

He shakes his head. Something not quite right about this particular story. He'll just take it out of the typewriter, set it aside, and work on it later.

If the walls of her box were any higher, Molly would be climbing them. *What are you doing! Put that paper back and let me get out!* All to no avail as Happy Jack puts in a new sheet for a new story. She continues fuming, pouting, stomping, and storming until further notice.

Dueling Duo

Happy Jack is ready for thrill-a-minute-action! Look at those typewriter keys fly! And look at Larry and Wally dash onto stage, engaged in an embittered duel to the death with flashing sabres. They dodge, dive, thrust, deflect, leap! Lookout Hollywood, here comes Happy Jack! The duelists fight over the head of Happy Jack, but he doesn't notice. They leap over the table!

Lookout! They messed up a stack of papers on the table and Happy Jack pauses to tidy it up. The duelists use this moment to catch their breath and wipe the sweat from their brows.

Papers tidied, the typing and swordfighting resume with renewed frenzy. Happy Jack bites his tongue and . . . Wally slips backwards, falls to the floor, drops his sword, and looks up to find Larry poised, ready to deliver the final thrust. Wally gulps and shuts his eyes in preparation for the final moment.

Happy Jack stops and gulps, too. *This is good stuff! Whew!* He reaches over and pours himself a glass of water. *Got to think carefully and not get swept away. How am I going to do this?*

Larry continues to stand over Wally with a big grin on his face. He's looking forward to his ultimate victory and enjoys seeing Wally squirm. Wally on the other hand . . . is tired of squirming. He motions, he *pleads* for Happy Jack to make it quick.

Happy Jack sets his glass down. *I've got it!* His fingers step into high gear and . . .

Wally smiles! He quickly pulls a gun out of his pocket and shoots Larry in the heart. Larry stumbles backwards and turns to Happy Jack. *Thanks, pal, I really appreciate that.* Larry can be *so* sarcastic.

Happy Jack frowns. *It looks okay to me, but will it sell in Hoboken?* He shrugs with indifference, tears the paper out of the typewriter, crumples and tosses it over his shoulder. Larry and Wally do a fair imitation of being crumpled and tossed by contorting their bodies and spinning and tumbling offstage.

Dueling of a Different Dimension

Happy Jack puts a clean sheet of paper into the typewriter. He's almost exhausted after that fast-paced action passage. He's ready for something more . . . *soft*. He smiles. *And pleasant.* He smiles wider and his eyes look far, far away. *Yes, very, very pleasant.*

Behind him, Molly starts yelling with renewed vigor. Happy Jack winces and turns around. *Knock it off, would you? I'm trying to concentrate!* She has no intention of knocking it off, thank you, not until she's out of that !*#*! box!

Happy Jack smirks. He pulls out the blank sheet of paper and puts in the one describing Molly's predicament. Molly nods her head. *That's more like it, you knuckle cracking knucklehead!* He begins typing. *Hey, what are you doing? What kind of a sicko are you, anyway?*

That's not . . . But she can say no more. Her mouth is clamped tight and her arms bound in straightjacket.

Reinserting the clean sheet . . .

Matchmaker, Matchmaker

Happy Jack begins typing, not quickly, but smoothly, confidently. He raises his eyebrow now and then, like a man of the world seducing a young innocent. He cocks his head and smiles slowly. *Think again, my little fawn. Do not resist your animal instinct. Do you really wish to say you do not wish to drink at the babbling brook with one such as I?*

WHACK! Carla slaps Larry in the face and he tumbles onto the stage with the scorned woman hot on his tail. Happy Jack slams the exclamation point home with fervor.

She's mad and doesn't mince around. *You? And me? Ha!* It's obvious she's lost count of how many steps above Larry she considers herself to be. Larry stands and gently puts his hand on her shoulder. She swats it away, turns her back on him, and folds her arms.

Larry throws his arms high. *Please, please, please!*

Happy Jack stops. A writers writes from experience, and Happy Jack just doesn't have that much, especially when it comes to getting beautiful women to change their minds on the matter of a harmless dalliance. He calls Larry, equally, if not more frustrated, over for a man-to-man conference. They huddle and confer. Happy Jack suggests Larry remove a certain ring from a certain finger and try again. *Why not?*

Larry returns to Carla's side. He whispers into her ear as she remains unmoving. But what's this? Has he found the right words? Is she indeed smiling, turning with open arms? You bet!

But hold everything! Happy Jack stops typing again. He picks up the ring and looks at Larry. Happy Jack scowls. Is he disgusted with Larry for playing around behind someone's back, or is he jealous that he's not in Larry's shoes at this moment?

Larry and Carla turn to Happy Jack. They're both caught in the fervor of the moment and would like things to continue at the normal pace . . . FAST! But when Happy Jack begins typing, they each roll their eyes in frustration and back away from each other. Enter fat, bungling Wally, who takes Carla in his arms and begins kissing her. Carla groans. *YIK!* She doesn't like this, but what can she do? She doesn't have the typewriter.

Powerless

Speaking of typewriters, Happy Jack, who's been typing rather wildly and carelessly, doesn't realize that his machine has been moving slowly to the edge of the table. Before he realizes what's happening, the typewriter falls to the floor. *Darn!* He bends to pick it up and sees that he has been joined by Larry, Carla, and Molly, all of whom are now free of his control. Only Wally, cheated out of some serious kissing, is alone, pouting.

Happy Jack looks up. *Er, something I can do for you folks?* They glare at him and Happy Jack looks a little bit frightened. He nervously puts the typewriter back on the table and tries to type them back to where they belong. Molly laughs. She steps around and picks up the disconnected plug from the floor.

Happy Jack gulps. *Um, yeah, uh, gee, look at the time! Guess I'd better be going.* He picks up his papers and walks across the stage to exit.

Molly smiles again. She plugs the typewriter in. Carla sticks in a piece of paper. Larry begins typing. And Wally, now with the group, returns the carriage at the proper moments. Happy Jack promptly walks back on stage, albeit a tad stiffly and without his usual smile. The Gang of Four turn to him. *They* smile.

Larry cracks his knuckles and flexes his fingers. *Let's see, where shall we begin?*

Molly Says:

Every performance is fun, but sheesh! What a relief when it's over! Here's a nice way to wrap things up, not only for you and your audience, but for us and our readers. Hope you've had fun! Say hello when we meet down the road, okay? Till then . . .

The Thank-You Artists

Scratchpad

Holding a large sketchbook (a real one, about 26" x 30"), Molly walks onto the stage with her head in the air. Is she something of a snob? No, she's watching the birds and butterflies and clouds and drawing pictures of them in her book. She's having a grand time.

Also walking across the stage with his head in the air is Larry, who, in fact, is indeed something of a snob. CRASH! They bump into each other and land on their bottoms. Molly's a little disoriented and wonders if she should be angry with this character. Larry sniffs and turns his head. He's not angry. He's grown accustomed to the fact that everyone else in the world isn't as bright as he is and occasionally commits stupid blunders.

They get to their feet and start to walk away when Larry notices the sketchpad. *Er, say, are you an artist?*

Molly blushes like a schoolgirl. She grins nervously and holds her hands wide. *Well, kinda . . . I guess. Sure.*

Larry suggest that she draw a portrait of his face. Molly's mouth drops open. *Really? Me? You? You'd want me to? Okay!*

Three's a Crowd

Molly no sooner starts drawing than Carla walks up behind her. One look at the sketchpad and she breaks into ringing peals of laughter. Larry comes over to investigate. He looks at the pad and can't see any humor. He explains: *Why, that's me! Perfect!*

Carla looks at him for the first time. Why, so it is! Again she is unable to control her laughing. Larry steps back and fingers his chin and nose uncertainly.

After laughing, Carla comes up with an idea for a drawing. She points forward, towards the audience. *What do you think, Molly? Think that'd make a good drawing?*

Molly doesn't know, but she'll sure give it her best. A doodle here, a squiggle there. No, cautions Larry, now back in the action, *a doodle there, a squiggle here!* Carla scoffs. *You mean a doodle there and two squiggles here!* Molly tries to follow their instructions while studying the audience. Her penciling and erasing proceed furiously.

And Four's a Team

In moments they realize the drawing simply isn't working. *It's not relevant,* says Carla. *It's not classical,* says Larry. *It's not fun,* says Molly. They return their studious stares to the audience after a collective sigh.

Things perk up, however, when Wally joins them. *Hey, whatcha making? Oh, pretty neat.* He looks at the audience, then at the drawing. *Maybe just a squiggle or two here, one there, and a doodle'll do.*

Larry and Carla are leary of accepting new advice, but Molly figures she has nothing to lose.

WOW! PERFECT! WILL YOU LOOK AT THAT!

Everyone agrees the drawing is complete. Wally urges Molly to turn the drawing over and show the audience, but she's embarrassed. Carla gives her a nudge. Quite bored with this silly bickering, he takes the pad out of Molly's hands and turns over the first sheet. The audience reads:

T H A N K   Y O U !

Wally takes it in his hands and turns over the next sheet:

A N D

He scratches his head and frowns. What's that supposed to mean? Molly and Carla both take the pad and turn over the final sheet:

GOODBYE!

They take a final bow as the lights fade to black.

ABOUT THE AUTHOR

Mime artists evolve from many different theatrical starting points. As you may guess from the name "Happy Jack," author Happy Jack Feder's path into mime art began with juggling, clowning and puppeteering. These arts are so closely related that one can quickly see why Happy Jack is such an exceptionally versatile performer. His mime performances have a wider range than that of the specialist mime.

In addition to performing, Happy Jack Feder is an author of performing arts books: *Clown Skits for Everyone* preceded this book and certainly there will be more to come.

Happy Jack is married with a daughter. The Happy Jack Feders live in Montana.

If you liked MIME TIME, you'll also want Happy Jack Feder's other book:

CLOWN SKITS FOR EVERYONE

by Happy Jack Feder

Everything you need to know to be a performing clown — written by a performing clown! Advice and ideas plus thirty-two easy-to-perform skits for one or two clown acts. Talks about gestures and actions, rehearsals and routines, talking or miming, modifying skits and the mechanics of performance. Tells about how to make props and the best techniques for beginners. All of the thirty-two skits included in the book have been performance-tested — simplified for easy memorization. The book is delightfully illustrated throughout by Lafe Locke.

Paperback book (192 pages) ISBN 0-916260-75-5

ORDER FORM

mp

MERIWETHER PUBLISHING LTD.
P.O. BOX 7710
COLORADO SPRINGS, CO 80933
TELEPHONE: (719) 594-4422

Please send me the following books:

_____**Mime Time #TT-B101** $10.95
by Happy Jack Feder
A book of mime routines and performance tips

_____**The Mime Book #TT-B124** $10.95
by Claude Kipnis
A comprehensive guide to the art of mime

_____**Clown Skits for Everyone #TT-B147** $9.95
by Happy Jack Feder
A delightful guide to becoming a performing clown

_____**Clown Act Omnibus #TT-B118** $10.95
by Wes McVicar
Everything you need to know about clowning

_____**Learning With Puppets #TT-B136** $6.95
by Hans and Karl Schmidt
An illustrated guide to making puppets in the classroom

_____**Comedy Improvisation #TT-B175** $9.95
by Delton T. Horn
Improv structures and exercises for young actors

*I understand that I may return any book
for a full refund if not satisfied.*

NAME: _____

ORGANIZATION NAME: _____

ADDRESS: _____

CITY: _____ STATE: _____ ZIP: _____

PHONE: _____

☐ **Check Enclosed**
☐ **Visa or Mastercard #** _____
                                    Expiration
Signature: _____ *Date:* _____
          (required for Visa/Mastercard orders)

COLORADO RESIDENTS: Please add 3% sales tax.
SHIPPING: Include $1.50 for the first book and 50¢ for each additional book ordered.

☐ *Please send me a copy of your complete catalog of books and plays.*